Endorsements

Tapestry: The Divine Design for your Life is an encouraging book about Christine Tracy's discovery of the goodness of God. Her journey is compelling, as the reader is drawn into the same process. This book is a tapestry of the unique aspects of the Christian walk, woven and simplified into a loving invitation to go farther and to trust deeper. The author's courage becomes evident quite quickly as this kind of life clearly involves risk. But as in all things "kingdom," the rewards far outshine whatever level of risk we once felt was so intimidating. Christine not only has a story to tell, she generously shares the insights God has given through the process. And we, the readers, are richer because of it.

—Bill Johnson
Bethel Church, Redding, CA
Author of When Heaven Invades Earth
and Hosting His Presence

Christine uses the alphabet like artists use a brush, filling the pages with delightful, yet deeply meaning experiences that resonate from her life's journey and impact her readers. She awakens the unique and creative ways inside each person, so that they can appreciate and understand how they uniquely were created. If you want to find out your destiny and discover God's creative nature inside of you, READ this book. As she shares principles on God's nature and His ways, she is opening up a door for you to see the Father's love in a greater depth and hue. I would highly recommend this book for the seekers and the dreamers inside of us, who want to know that God really IS as good as He says He is.

—*Theresa Dedmon,*
Creative Arts Pastor and Overseer,
Bethel Church, Redding, Ca.

Chris Tracy's book, *Tapestry*, is a sweet collection of her life that has been gathered together like keep-sakes, little bits of precious moments, written on scraps of paper just waiting to be unveiled at the right moment in time. Chris opens up her heart to the ups and downs of her life as only she can, allowing God to work in all situations of her life. You will find yourself connecting with her heartfelt stories as you laugh and possibly shed a tear, because her story may just sound like your own.

—*Kathy Vallotton, Co-founder*
Bethel School of Supernatural Ministry,
Redding, California

Whether your faith gives you immense joy, or if you have doubts, questioning how much or even why God loves you, or you are wondering where He is when you need Him, *Tapestry* is a must read! Chris Tracy shares her amazing relationship with God. You'll feel as though she is sitting next to you as she tells of her many life-changing experiences that have happened simply by putting her faith in God. She offers insight and encouragement for everyone who picks up this book. God's love is genuine and He is always present!

—*DB Daugherty, Tabernash, Colorado*
Family Reunion Specialist
YMCA of the Rockies – Snow Mountain Ranch

Tapestry

Tapestry

*The Divine
Design for Your Life*

Christine Tracy

TATE PUBLISHING
AND ENTERPRISES, LLC

Published by Tate Publishing & Enterprises, LLC
127 E. Trade Center Terrace | Mustang, Oklahoma 73064 USA
1.888.361.9473 | www.tatepublishing.com

Tate Publishing is committed to excellence in the publishing industry. The company reflects the philosophy established by the founders, based on Psalm 68:11,
"The Lord gave the word and great was the company of those who published it."

Book design copyright © 2013 by Tate Publishing, LLC. All rights reserved.
Cover design by Joel Uber
Interior design by Caypeeline Casas
Cover photography by Christine Tracy

Published in the United States of America

ISBN: 978-1-62295-762-0
1. Religion / Christian Life / General
2. Religion / Christian Life / Personal Growth
13.03.01

Dedication

To my children, Rob, Rusty, Erin, and Bess: Thank you for the adventures you've allowed me to share with you, and for making me a mom and a grandma. I love you all so much, and I dedicate this, my first book, to you.

Table of Contents

Acknowledgments 11

Preface 13

Introduction... 15

Hues of Love 19

Tapestry 25

The Loom 31

The Blank Canvas 41

The Artist's Voice... 47

The Design and Designer 65

River Dance.. 75

The Golden Thread 95

The Scarlet Fiber... 105

The Painter's Perspective 115

The Finishing Touches 121

The Masterpiece.. 137

The Gallery 161

You Were Born to Create.. 177

Inheritance of Inspiration 185

Miracles—He is Still Creating 199

God's Wall of Fame 219

Appendix 1 225

Appendix 2: Books and Resources 229

Appendix 3 231

Endnotes 233

Acknowledgments

To DB Daugherty and Erin Toft: Thank you for your editing help, suggestions, and encouragement.

To Leslie Taylor: You are an amazing editor and friend.

To my writing partner, Dana Carey: Our books are nearly ready. Thanks for keeping me on target!

To Kathy Vallotton: You are an amazing and powerful woman. Thank you for your support, and many thanks to both you and your husband, Kris, for your sacrifices in creating and parenting the Bethel School of Supernatural Ministry.

To Bethel Senior Pastor Bill Johnson: Thank you for blessing my writing and encouraging me to make a book. Because of you, I have learned to dream with God.

To Theresa Dedmon: You validated the artist in me and set her free. Thank you.

To my husband, Rick: You always keep me laughing. You never allow me to take myself too seriously, and that made it possible for me to finish my first book. I love you!

To my Creator God: You are the best person I know. Always good. Always kind. Always there. Always happy. I can't wait to see how You and I take on the last third of my life

Preface

Dear Reader,

This book is a journey into relationship with me. I invite you to sit at my antique oak table and enjoy a steaming mug of coffee with cream and honey. You are special to me. I hope my stories bring you comfort, encouragement, and hope. If you hunger to know more of God; if you wonder about the supernatural; if you long to understand how much He loves you; if you are helping a friend know more about God, Jesus, and Holy Spirit; if you are young and yearn for an understanding heart to help you make sense of your life; then I feel God has put this book in your hands for such a time as this.

May His anointing be on these words, and may you sense His love with you as you read.

Love,
Chris

P.S. At the end of each chapter there are blessings and reflections to guide your journey through this book. I encourage you to keep a journal close by. If you have never given your life to God, I invite you to say a simple prayer of salvation located at the end of this book. This is part of the journey and will help you understand the secrets and treasures that are about to be unveiled to you.

Introduction

An artist starts with a blank canvas, an array of brushes, a palette of paints, and a glimmer of an idea.

A musician hears a tune in his head and finds it on the strings of his instrument.

A weaver strings his loom, and imagines color and texture as he works the pattern.

A writer enters a place in her heart where the brain doesn't hinder and where words and poetry are born.

A photographer looks through a lens to frame the soul of her subject.

A jeweler looks lovingly at the metal and stone and sees the final beauty before he begins.

A sculptor chooses a perfect piece of marble and, like Michelangelo, chips away until his subject is set free.

A stained glass craftsman sees in his mind's eye the end from the beginning, wondering how the light will hit each facet of this magnificent reflection of his passion.

A master chef uses all her senses to make her culinary creation, carefully selecting each ingredient and combining them to meet the taste, look, texture, and aroma that will arouse the senses of the partaker.

And the Divine Artist—who created the universe and is *still* creating—once took up His tools of love, passion, color, and substance and made you. He thought up what would make you different from every other human: personality, character, appearance, gifting, ability, and purpose. "Let us create man in our image," they said (Father, Son and Holy Spirit), and they gave you a portion of their own divine life and imagination. You were created to be creative—thinking and moving with God.

You are way more than you think you are.

The ups and downs, crises and fun times, sad and happy experiences, your dreams and goals, relationships and thoughts are all part of the tapestry of your life. The dark times contrast the bright times, making them more beautiful. The high places wouldn't be so lovely without the low places. Like a mountain wildflower that can only exist in extreme weather areas, you are an exquisite creation that is becoming more beautiful as the years and experiences go by.

As you read this book, you will discover your own life's design, and learn new things about your Creator, whose light invades your darkness and whose imagination has fashioned you to be unique and amazing.

Are you ready to discover what God had in mind when He imagined you?

> I want you woven into a tapestry of love, in touch with everything there is to know of God. Then you will have minds confident and at rest, focused on Christ, God's great mystery. All the richest treasures of wisdom and knowledge are embedded in that mystery and nowhere else.
>
> Colossians 2:1-3 (The Message)

Hues of Love

I lift up my eyes to the mountains—
where does my help come from?
My help comes from the Lord,
the Maker of heaven and earth.
He will not let your foot slip—
he who watches over you will not slumber;
indeed, he who watches over Israel
will neither slumber nor sleep.
The Lord watches over you—
the Lord is your shade at your right hand;
the sun will not harm you by day,
nor the moon by night.
The Lord will keep you from all harm—
he will watch over your life;
the Lord will watch over your coming and going
both now and forevermore.

Psalm 21 (NIV)

May 2010

It's a rare cloudy and hot afternoon in the mountains of Colorado.

Rick and I have just gone through a transition of gigantic proportions, or should I say we *are* going through it. It isn't over. It may not be over in three months. It may not be over in a year. It may never be over.

Here we are in a new, pretty apartment. It's cute on the inside—small, bright, and cheery—and it fits my wonderful, friendly furniture. On the outside, it looks somewhat like a warehouse in the middle of a large dirt parking lot. If I look beyond the cars and the fences and the buildings, I can make out the Indian Peaks of the Continental Divide. If I look south, there is Eagles Nest Peak and the snow-covered mountains that make up the Gore Range. These mountains are also visible from distant towns that sit in other directions, including Winter Park, Vail, Breckenridge, Dillon, Silverthorne, and Keystone.

Rick is on the fifth day of his new job as a yard-man at a local lumber company and hardware store. His wages are minimal compared to what he used to bring home. We are really starting over. This time, however, there is no striving, no stress, no anxiety, no urgency, no upset stomachs and sleepless nights, and no irate phone calls. This job is his healing job. I pray he is able to remember why he loves the smell of wood, the feel of a hammer, and the friendly quips of passing carpenters and home-improvement hobbyists.

We are now back in our hometown of Kremmling after a year of ministry school, and we are being happily welcomed by old friends. Our delight in seeing our family is blessed especially by the chance to cuddle six-month-old Mesa, who we haven't seen since her fifth day of life.

The difficulties and heartaches of the last few years have not reared their ugly heads as we had expected. No one has said a word to remind us. Are they being careful to not hurt our feelings or drum up sadness? Maybe. But more than anything, our friends and family are genuinely happy to have us home. We are consumed in love—more than enough of it. And all we feel for them and for the people of our town is love.

It's a love that was increased at ministry school where we learned for the first time just how much God loves us. There's a song we sang there about how wide and deep and high the love of God is. Oh, how I wanted to understand that love when I first set foot in this wild school of supernatural life that was filled with students of a younger generation.

God knew I had that in my heart. He heard my cry. He saw my pain. He lifted me. Set me on His lap. Kissed my forehead. Held me in His arms. And He laughed over me.

He laughed!

And I laughed, too. In that joy was all the love of a Papa who is proud of His child. He thinks I'm smart. Even funny! He loves me where I am. He loves me even though I haven't always been the perfect daughter.

His love has no boundaries and no conditions. He calls me *friend*.

He is a happy, good God who loves to dance and sing over me. He is for me, and not against me. He has orchestrated a wonderful life for me. He sees the end from the beginning. He calls His creation (me!) good, and He wants me to enjoy His kingdom—full of peace, joy, and righteousness. How can I resist such a Person? How can I reject such a love?

I can't. All I want is to know how I can love Him back. I want to somehow understand the depth of this great love.

On one of the first days of our ministry school experience, Rick and I were walking from the parking lot into Bethel Church in Redding, California (the home church of our Bethel School of Supernatural Ministry). Our new friend Giovanni, his wife, Stephanie, and their two children waved as they passed us in their car. When I smiled and waved, something filled me with such passion that I could hardly keep from crying. "I am in love with that family," I told Rick after they passed. I had never felt that way toward people before, especially people I didn't know well. And then God reminded me I had asked Him how I could love Him the way He loved me. His answer? "Beloved, you love Me when you love My children."

So began a journey over several months where God expanded my heart, my compassion, and my love by filling me with His heart, compassion and love.

When we were in Tijuana in the spring of 2010, ministering in tiny, extremely poor neighborhood churches, I once again felt that compelling love as I looked at a young girl. She was about ten, and half of her face was disfigured. But, oh, she was beautiful to me. I prayed for her, and I told her in complete honesty that she was a beautiful child. God didn't heal her face, but He changed something in me through that experience.

Love truly is the most important thing we, as followers of Jesus, can carry to a desperately hurting world.

If I had only learned one thing this year, understanding how much God loves me would have been more than enough. Yet, He chose to teach me so much more.

So Rick and I are back home now, starting over with new jobs and a living situation that is the result of great economic loss in 2008–2009. We're almost sixty. Most people in this world would look at our situation as pretty hopeless, but we don't. We have a God we trust, and we have faith for what's ahead. We know God is real and have testimony after testimony of how He has blessed us. We have even longer lists of miracles He's allowed us to witness and participate in. We sense His favor over our lives. He has given us really good friends, a family who loves us, and a church that recognizes God's hand in our lives. We are safe and protected under His wing. He has set us on a rock. He has proven Himself to be good in every way. How can we lose? There is so much more coming to us, and I can't wait to see what God is going to do.

You may be looking at your life and wondering how you will ever piece it back together. You may be just starting out, the whole world before you, with opportunity knocking. You may be sad over lost love. You, like me, may have been jolted by economic trouble. You may be wondering if your children are ever going to make it in life. You may be trying to navigate a situation that seems hopeless. Please don't feel alone. I don't know one person whose life is perfect.

Let me show you a way out of the mire and into hope.

As you read this book, may these words become your words, and my hope, your hope. As you discover more about you and your life, you will discover your own creativity emerging to partner with the Creator as He seeks to express Himself to you and through you to those you influence.

It's a grand adventure.

A Blessing for You

I bless you as you read this book, to be able to open your spirit to God's spirit, and to discover a new way to think and feel about your life.

Reflect and Receive

1. Consider your life today. Think about how you felt when you woke up this morning. Were you full of joy and anticipation at the new day? Were you worried or anxious? Write down how you felt in a journal you will keep while you read this book.

Tapestry

"Let us make man in Our image, according to Our likeness…"

Genesis 1:25-27 (NKJV)

Spring, 1961

Kiki dropped her hula-hoop and ran past her dad's prize tulips to the edge of the backyard where pink crabapple blossoms cascaded over the white picket fence. Beyond the gate, her friend, Liz, passed on the sidewalk, walking home from school. Kiki waved to her and ran back to her hula-hoop.

"One, two, three…" She could almost get up to 100. In fact, she was the regular winner at the summer block events that sometimes included turtle races, jacks, and summer theatre.

She could hear her parents inside with Grandpa and the minister. The Lord's Prayer floated quietly through the open sunroom window.

"Our Father, who art in heaven…"

Moments earlier, she had heard Reverend Hogue reading a Psalm about valleys, still waters, and death. The reverend came often these days to check up on Grandpa. Kiki and her brother, Chip, were usually sent outside or to their rooms when he visited.

Kiki swallowed back the ache in her throat, trying not to cry. She knew Grandpa was sick. She told God she loved her grandpa and asked Him to take care of him and help her mom be happy again.

Kiki tried to be good these days, offering to help in cleaning the dishes, ironing, or playing games with Grandpa, who now lived down the hall in what used to be her little brother's room. Mom seemed far away lately, and Kiki found herself growing inward, daydreaming and playing in a land where colors were bright, the sky was blue, and people were always happy.

———◆———

I think it was during this time that I, Kiki, started my journey with God. Though I really didn't know Him or understand much about Him, I knew somehow that there was more to my life than I could see. I knew God was somewhere in the scent of my dad's American Beauty roses. I sensed His presence when I gazed over the breezy bluffs of Lake Michigan. I felt His warmth in the sun at Atwater Beach. His love was in my grandmother's tight hugs, and His joy was in my grandpa's twinkling, blue eyes that always seemed to hide a special secret for me.

The Journey

In 1961, I was only ten years old. Now, in the spring of 2010, I am fifty-eight, and my journey with God has taken me from that quaint, white, Cape-Cod-style home across from Lake Bluff Elementary School in Shorewood, Wisconsin, to other places and adventures. It's been fun, sad, hard, easy, colorful, dangerous, exciting, loving, scary, devastating, purposeful, accidental, funny, dizzying, frustrating, lonely, happy, full of children, and totally fulfilling. And it's not finished yet.

When I look over the rollercoaster ride that is my life, I see a golden thread in a tapestry of color and texture that is woven into a work of art that could only have one Creator.

The artist is a living God. He's the painter, potter, sculptor, weaver, writer, composer, and friend.

This is what I want to help you understand about your own life.

Can you see your tapestry? Can you feel it? Does your heart recite your poetry? Do your innermost thoughts recognize the Master's touch?

Made in His Image

We are created in the image of God. We are His art, and we are created to be creative like Him. Not only that, our very *life* is God's creation. He sees the finished piece and knows what He has created us to do. He has woven a destiny for us that is good and unique and that only we are specifically designed to fulfill.

Do you know what's ahead for you? God does. Can you see the piece of art your life is? God can. Do you want to discover what is ahead? God wants you to. Is it possible to see it? I'll try to help you—with God's assistance.

Remember how God specifically gave instructions to His handpicked craftsmen in the Bible? His colors were exact. His measurements were precise. He gave detailed guidelines about which precious metals, woods, and gemstones were to be used for the building of His tabernacle.

The earth, the sun, the moon, and the universe are still being created. The inherent beauty of nature is designed specifically to point us to the Creator. The stars in the sky shout His glory and reality.

"The heavens declare the glory of God; the skies proclaim the work of his hands" (Psalm 19:1).

And what about His most beloved creation—human beings? Man and woman were beautifully made in the image of God, His Son, and His Spirit. He made us to be a physical, emotional, spiritual masterpiece, each of us reflecting a unique aspect of God's character.

If God is so specific and intentional about His beloved human creation, could it also be true that He *continues* to fashion a purpose in us as we walk out our lives with Him?

Look at your life from heaven's viewpoint. Consider your family, your grandparents, your experiences, the good and the hard. Find the golden thread that connects the years of your life as you have walked through it with God. See the tapestry? Is there texture? Rub your hands over the colorful piece. Can you feel the high places and the low places?

Is it finished yet? No. He's not done yet. Not if you're still alive.

If you are searching, but not sure what's ahead, and don't even know how to pray about it, you are not alone. But understand that your life has not been a mistake. There is a design, and it even includes the grace God extended for the times you walked away from Him, forgiveness for the times you were not obedient, His protection during times of trouble, and a red under-pattern that anchors your life in all that Christ paid for on the cross.

Your story has bestseller promise. Your tapestry could hang in the finest art museum. You may not know the end yet, but God does. He promises:

> For I know the plans I have for you," declares the Lord, "plans to prosper you and not to harm you, plans to give you hope and a future.
>
> Jeremiah 29:11 (NIV)

A Blessing for You

I bless you with the ability to look at your life from God's perspective, to remember times God was with you, when He brought healing, gave you wisdom, answered your prayer, eased your loneliness, and poured His love into your hurting heart. May you remember good times of great blessing and joy; and intimately know your Father as your good and able Papa.

Reflect and Receive

1. Write about a time in your life when you sensed God for the first time.

2. Jesus went to the mountain to pray and meet with His Father. Where do you go to be alone with God?

3. Make a timeline or draw a picture of your life so far. Ask God to show you how He has been with you from the time you were born. When He brings a thought, write it down.

4. If you can see His hand in your life, start to be aware of the pattern of circumstances, opportunities, and experiences. Now project them forward in your life. What dreams or goals do you have in your heart? Can you trust your Papa to guide you?

The Loom

For you created my inmost being; you knit me
together in my mother's womb.

Psalm 139:13 (NIV)

My brother and sister-in-law used to have a large loom
taking over a spare bedroom in their home. It sat there
awhile, stretching a partially woven rug that was started
by the loom's original owner and never finished.

Looms are complicated, heavy, come in different sizes, and require a skill and language unique to
the weaver.

Words like *warping*, *shuttles*, *maple*, *beeswax*, and
fiber are all part of the jargon.

So how does a loom factor into the tapestry of life?
Just like a loom creates a foundation on which to weave,
our lives also have a foundation—the Creator.

God's Plan for You

God had a plan when He thought about you. Did you know you were on His mind before you took on physical form?

"Before I formed you in the womb I knew you, before you were born I set you apart" (Jeremiah 1:5).

He planned for you to be born to your specific parents, in your particular town and country, and in the birth order of your brothers and sisters. His blueprint even detailed your curly hair and taste for chocolate.

God in all His creativity, humor, and joy thought about you ahead of time. And He thought about everyone else He is ever going to create.

Have you heard of divine appointments? Even now He plans those, too. He also gives us a free choice of whether we will love and accept Him.

My journey from child to adult took a rather altered, confusing route as I searched for God. You will have your own stories. You may even be in the middle of your story. Following are some of my experiences that added dimension, color, and texture to my life's tapestry.

Imaginings

When I was little, I had a big imagination.

There was a plumbing access door in the wall next to my twin bed.

My room was pink, pretty, and frilly—thanks to Mom, who had an eye for decorating. Sometimes my grandma would come visit and sleep in the other twin bed in my room. I remember playing rummy up in my room with her—a special time for both of us.

Outside my windows were towering elm trees that swayed in the wind that came off of Lake Michigan. Summers were hot and humid, and my windows were always open, the ruffled white curtains waving with the shifts of hot and cool air. At night, I'd lay on top of my covers, just trying to cool down.

In my imaginings, I'd drum up very scary things at night. So fearsome that my Tiny Tears dolly was propped between me and that plumbing trap door. I was sure there were dark and evil things behind that door ready to grab me while I slept. My strategy was that they would take my doll instead. (Great "Mommy," huh?)

In those days, the television show *The Twilight Zone* provided family night entertainment on the big, boxy television that sat in a corner of our living room. I distinctly remember one black-and-white episode where a child "fell" through a time warp in a wall into the fourth dimension. Her family could hear her through their TV set but couldn't find her. She was alone and trapped in a colorless tangle of trails, tunnels, and cobwebs. This really scared me and fed my fears.

Other imaginings of mine included the giant albino spider that lived under my bed. I had a route through my bedroom, climbing from bed, to dresser, and then jumping out the door so my feet wouldn't touch the floor. This ensured escape from certain death if I had to use the bathroom.

At night when the lights were out, the moving tree branches, waving curtains, street lights, and passing car headlights all gave my room an eerie whirl of shadow and light. Sometimes the sights and sounds brought me comfort. Other times, though, the shadows frightened me enough to make me hide under the covers.

To add to my fright, I would remember a story my mom told me about a woman who lived in my room in the "olden days."

Mom would sit on the edge of my bed after tucking me in and saying prayers with me. She was funny. It was always a special time for me. I loved to hear her stories. One night she told me the true story of the spooky housekeeper.

My mom's mother died of spinal meningitis when Mom was a child. Because my grandfather was a salesman and often travelled, my mom and my aunt were raised by a series of live-in housekeepers in the same house where I grew up. Every night, a certain housekeeper would talk to her dead husband who came to visit at the second-floor bedroom window—*my bedroom window*. This anecdote would usually come in a string of stories that were both humorous and sad. But it's the one I remembered most.

I just couldn't get over thinking about the dead guy at the window. Morbid, I know. If Mom had only known.

The '70s

In the '70s, when I was in my twenties, my curiosity about faith and religion piqued. My days at North

Shore Presbyterian Church were long over, and I pretty much forgot what I learned there.

College "intellectualized" me. I learned to think for myself, and my reasoning and logic made me feel pretty sure about what I believed. My German grandma on my dad's side taught me about yoga, Eastern philosophy, swamis, and ancient religions. I idolized my grandma (still love and miss her), and I loved visiting her and rereading her long letters to me that were filled with philosophy and teaching. I think my parents were hesitant about what she was telling me but offered little to counter it. I don't think they knew what to say to this rebellious and worldly young daughter. They just loved me and kept encouraging me in whatever I was pursuing, which I am thankful for to this day.

The Jesus Movement

The Jesus Movement had been spreading for a few years, but it repulsed me. An old boyfriend called one day when I was in my dorm at college. He was in Wisconsin, and I was now living in Missouri. He said he was worried about me and tried to convert me on the phone. "Don't you love Jesus? You should go to a Jesus meeting!" This discussion with him made me feel sick, and I hung up. It was a long time before we spoke again.

I determined to cross the street any time a Jesus freak would look as if he was going to talk to me. They all reminded me of the strange, ragged people in my childhood memories who would stand on the corners of downtown Milwaukee holding signs declaring "The end of the world is near!"

New Age

A few years later—still on my quest for spiritual truth—I was primed and ready when a group of people I worked with at a ski lodge in Colorado invited me to join a New Age metaphysical study group. We read and we prayed and we chanted. I felt part of something important. We were taught that we were God. And because of that we were a force. We had power. We could heal people and change circumstances. We had readings done by palm readers and psychics who were connected to spirit guides who could tell our future and tell us who we were created to be. The elements of the earth, like crystals and rainbows, were holy and brought good luck. Though some Native American and eastern religions were respected, as well as Christian Science, Jesus the Christ was never mentioned, nor was the one God who created the universe honored. We didn't worship the God who lives in us, but the god or divine energy who *is* us.

It was philosophical and intellectual, and it fascinated me. We were seekers after truth, trying to explain our existence and understand what was real and what was not. We meditated and sought out-of-body experiences, finding our own spirit guides. We sometimes rejected mainstream medicine and went after an alternative, holistic lifestyle.

I loved the people in the group. They were so real, so loving, and so caring. The philosophy we studied and the supernatural life that came out of it were so compelling. And what sealed the deal for me was the tangible electric power we all felt when we joined hands and chanted. Wow. I didn't think then about the fact that the universal intelligence we recognized was not the same as the God of my childhood.

Then one night, I was at my apartment where I lived with my big, white Great Pyrenees dog, Brutus. I was meditating cross-legged on the floor when suddenly an eerie presence seemed to be right outside my windows. I looked outside and could see nothing but the darkness of a huge meadow against a black sky, but I felt like there were many things out there ready to take my life. A chilling fear gripped me, and it increased when Brutus stepped to the window and growled. He saw something.

I knew what I was sensing was evil. I didn't know what to do. My dog and I just hunkered down and made it through the night. But the following morning, I asked my friend, who was one of the leaders of our study group, what she thought my experience was all about.

She shrugged nonchalantly and said, "When those things happen, just say the Lord's Prayer, and they will go away."

I was shocked. I thought if God, the Father of Jesus, is the one with the ultimate power, then what am I doing messing with a counterfeit?

I remembered the Lord's Prayer. In fact, I had said it every night in years past. I also remembered the words I had spoken at my Presbyterian church—The Apostle's

Creed—a declaration of what I should have believed, but never quite grasped. (See Appendix 3.)

My friends wondered why I never returned to the study group. Soon my heart, soul, and mind were on a quest to find the one true God—the one I knew as a child. Would He want me? How would I find Him? What about the wild life I was living? What was He thinking? What was my life for? Questions came flooding into my mind. It would still be a long time before I would find Him.

Yet, He was always right there.

The loom that will host your tapestry is the knowledge that the Father created you, designed you, formed you, was excited by you, loved you, and wanted you way before you were conceived.

In the next chapter, we will prepare the foundation of His love upon the loom of your life.

A Blessing for You

Friend, I bless you to be able to know the truth about God that sets you free; to understand with your mind the wisdom that is yours in Him; to believe in the unseen reality of God's protection over you in the experiences of your life; to discover your true Foundation that is the God who created you. He is unmoving and always good.

Reflect and Receive

1. How have your experiences shaped your life?
2. How are you different from your friends, based on some of those experiences?
3. Name a time when you were led astray or deceived about your beliefs. How did you find the truth?
4. What are some things you dream about for the future?

The Blank Canvas

Lord, you have been our home since the beginning. Before the mountains were born and before you created the earth and the world, you are God. You have always been, and you will always be.

Psalm 90:1-2 (NCV)

The West Grand High School track is just a stone's throw from my 2010 summer apartment in Kremmling, Colorado.

It quietly beckons me every morning as I think up all sorts of excuses not to go walk: *I have to do my reading. Bath time is next. Now the bed needs to be made, the bills need to be paid, and I have to catch up with my daugh-*

*ter in Boulder. I need to start working on the church news-
letter. And there is editing to do. I promised myself I would
update my website. And what about the online organization I applied for? I never received an answer. Better check
on that.*

As the minutes slip by, and the day heats up, I realize it's just too hot to walk around that sunbathed track.
My day is full, and so is my body—with snacks and
stuff that is definitely not what I need to get healthy.

But on the days when I get out in the cool of the
morning, when the sunlight rays begin to color the
nearby cliffs, and the birds are singing, "Oh," I say out
loud to myself, "why don't I do this every day?"

I always feel good when I walk around that soft, red
asphalt. I revel in the views of the snowy peaks of the
Eagles' Nest Wilderness to the south, the Indian Peaks
of the Continental Divide to the east, the striking
Gore Canyon of the Colorado River to the west, and
the ruggedly beautiful Kremmling cliffs to the north.
The morning air fills my lungs with something so pure,
while my body eases and relaxes, and I step out, smiling
greetings to other walkers.

What a way to start the day! I go round and round
as I pray for my children, grandchildren, husband, and
friends, thanking God in every sentence for His amazing grace and goodness. I declare His promises over my
life and those that I love, and I sing songs of praise as I
round the mile mark.

Why would I avoid this wonderful hour? I can think
of all sorts of ways to sabotage my health and happi-
ness. Why?

This is not unlike the excuses we make to avoid God's beckoning. He calls us to Himself. He is constantly speaking to us in all sorts of ways. Yet we cover our ears. We welcome the familiar busyness that is our comfort zone, and we decline to respond as He stands there with arms open wide and a smile of excitement, anticipating an amazing moment with His child.

Does God Really Talk to Us?

Do you know how God speaks to you? Have you heard His still, small voice or recognized His message in a thought or picture? Does His magnificent creation communicate to your spirit? What about your night dreams and daydreams?

He wants to show you His nature and His ways through His Word, your thoughts, and your friends.

He calls out, "Be still!"

Stop planning. End the busyness. Stop the voices that distract you. Turn off the lies that keep you from listening to the One who loves you and wants to give you so much.

One Cool September Morning

It took me a long time to learn that God really talks to me. About eight years ago on a September Sunday morning, I was lingering in morning sleep when I heard a whisper in my ear.

Go forward today for healing, the voice said.

I opened my eyes, and no one was there. I quickly let it go and fell back to sleep, and suddenly there it was again.

Chris, go forward today and ask for healing.

I opened my eyes and sat up. No one was around.

I climbed out of bed and got ready for church. While Rick and I drove the twelve miles to Kremmling Community Church, I told him about the whisper. We didn't discuss it further, but I knew I was not about to go forward in church. I had never done that before.

Still, I reasoned, my shoulder *is* hurting, *and I have been praying for God to take the pain away.*

We had a guest speaker that day. During worship and announcements, I kept wondering about the whisper. *Was that God?* I decided I probably had just imagined something.

Soon the guest pastor, in the middle of his sermon, looked right toward me and said, "If God is telling you to do something, you had better do it." My heart exploded. God had my attention.

After the service I told one of the elders of our church what I had heard in bed that morning, and he ushered me forward where three men—the guest pastor, the elder, and my husband, Rick—prayed for my healing. The pastor's hand grew hot when he put it on my shoulder, and pretty soon the pain was gone.

God healed me that day on so many levels. Stress was the ruler of my life during that time, with worries over my children, work, life, finances—just about everything. In short, I was not trusting in the God who was able to take care of me. That prayer of healing gave new life to my spirit, soul, and body in ways I never even asked for. God knew what I needed. He compelled me to come to Him. My excuses could not stand in the presence of His mighty purposes for me.

> Many are the plans in a man's heart, but it is the Lord's purpose that prevails.
>
> Proverbs 19:21 (NIV)

That whisper, my response, and His healing propelled me into a new life with Him that gave me hope in His power, confidence in His authority, peace in His purposes, rest in His love, and an awesome hunger and thirst for more of His glory in my life.

Thankfully, Rick, who had been praying for me with the group that morning, was touched in the same way I was, and at the same time. We were on a new journey to discover more of the nature of the One who loves us most.

Have you heard Him? Do you want to? Are you ready to respond to His heart for you?

The foundation fabric of your tapestry is His love for you. He's beckoning. He's waiting like a loving Father, kneeling down, arms wide, waiting for you to run and jump in abandon and trust for all He wants to give you.

He's calling. Will you come?

A Blessing for You

You are created by God with a capacity to hear His voice, know His desires for you, and have true and intimate friendship with Him. May you, in this week, discover new dimensions of this friendship and love with your Father. May you hear Him in the quiet and in the noise. May His spirit give voice to your own spirit, propelling you forward into your place of destiny.

Reflect and Receive

1. Have you ever had a dream or heard a voice and felt like God might be speaking through them? Write about it. Begin to keep a journal of dreams and experiences, praying that the Holy Spirit, Son, and Father will use them to reveal not only their nature, but also your destiny.

2. Are you beginning to see the tapestry of your own life? Can you see the foundation fabric of His love in your life experience so far?

The Artist's Voice

They shouted, "This is the voice of a God, not of a man."

Acts 12:22 (NIV)

Learning to Listen

It was July 2010, and my good friend Debbie was sitting across the table, smiling at me with big, blue eyes as we waited for our lunch. We've been friends since the early '80s, our kids grew up in the same schools, we worked together at Bible camp, and our husbands were friends, too.

While we were talking about her son attending the same ministry school my husband and I had attended, she blurted, "I see the word *go* in big letters on your forehead surrounded by a cloud!"

She was not aware of Rick's and my desire to return for a second year of ministry school, nor did she know about our uncertainty and the hard decisions that surrounded moving back to Redding, California.

I had been waiting for some clear signs from God as confirmation of what we were to do. *Was this it?* Rick and I had been praying, watching, and listening for answers, knowing that God does indeed communicate His purposes, ideas, and direction to us in ways He has equipped us to hear.

So this was huge! Debbie went on to tell me more of what she felt God was speaking to her. What an uplifting lunch date! What an encouragement. What a way to meet me in divine appointment.

The Symphony

God is always talking to us in many ways. He's big—bigger than we imagine. He's able to talk to all His children at once, and to commune and relate at any moment through His Son, Jesus, and through His Holy Spirit. Some people just hear a voice. Others, like Debbie, see images. Still others get thoughts.

It's important to discover how He speaks to us. We can do this by being still, listening, paying attention to thoughts that pop into our mind, being aware of colors and feelings around a person or situation, and giving attention to verses that seem to jump out of the Bible.

Following are just some of the ways we can hear from Him. I learned about many of these from reading *Dreaming With God* by Bill Johnson, Senior Pastor at Bethel Church in Redding, California. When I read the book, I realized God had been speaking to me all along in many ways in recent years. In hindsight, I remember many times in my life, even as a child, when He was trying to get my attention.

Still, Small Voice

I have heard the still, small voice of God twice in my life that I can remember. The first time was the time I mentioned earlier when He woke me up. This voice is one that you hear audibly, but people around you don't hear. You know that someone has spoken to you. It can be a whisper or a quiet voice or even maybe a loud voice. It can even be a direct thought. This voice is just for you.

The second time this happened to me was several years ago when I had a terrible car accident. It was March 17, 2003—St. Patrick's Day—and I was heading home alone after taking my daughter Bess to visit her older sister, Erin, at college in Wyoming. Light snow was falling, and it was getting dark as I came down off the pass that connects Laramie, Wyoming, and Walden, Colorado. In good weather, I was about an hour from home and, seeing the town of Walden about a mile ahead, decided I would stop at a gas station for coffee.

My eyes were heavy. My head was numb. And I fell asleep.

Suddenly, I was careening down a steep embankment, then up the other side of a culvert, and soon I was airborne.

My foot had relaxed on the accelerator, forcing it down. I crossed the road and only awoke when my car broke through a fence and started flying. It was an odd sensation—very quiet as I cruised in the air. I kept hearing the words "You're okay. You're okay. You're okay," and I relaxed as the car hit the ground and tumbled end for end through a rancher's field, landing on its top.

The ambulance crew feared for my life as we drove through a blizzard to the nearest hospital an hour away. I, on the other hand, was confident everything was going to be okay. There was some head and chest pain. I didn't answer my age correctly (I became ten years younger), and I learned later my vital signs were at dangerous levels. My husband was notified, and he gathered a few praying friends and waited at the hospital in Kremmling. Gradually, as the praying continued, the paramedics began to radio improved vital signs as we traveled on slowly through what now was a raging blizzard. The doctor was amazed and credited the prayer. I spent three days in cardiac intensive care with a bruised heart and lung, a broken sternum, and a concussion. Yes, there were injury and recovery issues, and yes, there was pain. I'm here to say today that I know God saved me out of that accident for a purpose.

I have fully recovered from that accident, but not without a burning in my heart to seek and know the One who allowed me to live.

And who was that voice that calmed me as my car toppled through the rancher's field? It could have been an angel. The Bible tells us we have angels (see Hebrews 1:14). Or it could have been God, Jesus, or the Holy Spirit. They are all as close as our breath.

> Are not all angels ministering spirits sent to serve those who will inherit salvation?
>
> Hebrews 1:14 (NIV)

> This is what God the Lord says—the Creator of the heavens, who stretches them out, who spreads out the earth with all that springs from it, who gives breath to its people, and life to those who walk on it.
>
> Isaiah 42:5 (NIV)

Audible Voice

My friend Paula hears God talk to her when she's trail running on the beautiful pathways behind her mountain home. God guides her on the trail, asks her to talk with others on the trail, and often tells her what to say to them. She amazes me whenever she relates a conversation, and I always wonder why my experience is so different. God reveals Himself in different ways to each of us.

Thoughts

Do you ever wonder where some of your thoughts come from? If it's a great idea, a blessing, a creative thought, or a piece of wisdom that you would never have thought of normally, there is a good possibility God is speaking to you through your thoughts. Pray and ask Him to help you discern His thoughts in you. You can also pray for wisdom. Remember, you have the mind of Christ. This means that, like Christ, you have the ability to think supernaturally.

> If any of you lacks wisdom you should ask God, who gives generously to all without finding fault, and it will be given to you.
>
> James 1:5 (NIV)

> The unspiritual self, just as it is by nature, can't receive the gifts of God's Spirit. There's no capacity for them. They seem like so much silliness. Spirit can be known only by spirit—God's Spirit and our spirits in open communion. Spiritually alive, we have access to everything God's Spirit is doing and can't be judged by unspiritual critics. Isaiah's question, "Is there anyone around who knows God's Spirit, anyone who knows what he is doing?" has been answered: Christ knows, and we have Christ's Spirit.
>
> 1 Corinthians 2:14-16
> (The Message Bible)

> But we have the mind of Christ.
>
> 1 Corinthians 2:16 (NIV)

Images

I see images lately—just since I've been at ministry school. The school taught us to take risks and speak what we thought we were seeing and hearing in the spirit, using words of encouragement and edification. We practiced calling out the gold in people—what we felt God had put into them.

This is called prophecy. The Apostle Paul says we should all ask for the gift of prophecy:

> Follow the way of love and eagerly desire the gifts of the Spirit, especially prophecy.
>
> 1 Corinthians 14:1 (NIV)

Recently, God gave me an image for a friend. He was walking with God, and God's great, big hand was resting on his shoulder. The word *rest* was very big over this image. I believed it was for my friend and the church he pastors. I did not really understand this image and simply gave it to him with the thought that God would show him the meaning.

I have also been learning about prophetic art. Using music, writing, dance, drama, and painting, God can express His nature through those of us who will release our creative gifts. I often send cards to friends and loved ones with my own photography, art, or poems. The cards are unique to each one and express His promises to them through my art and writing.

One day, I saw a big rainbow trout over a friend. Rainbows stand for God's promises and covenant. Fish speak of abundance, provision, and salvation. We can receive these images and then ask God to interpret their meaning. Often, He will. If not, we can ask the person God intended it for if it means anything to them. There are many resources available online and in books that explore the spiritual and prophetic meanings of images, dreams, numbers, colors, and objects.

It's fun to creatively encourage others, and it is always a blessing to them.

> In the last days, God says, I will pour out my Spirit on all people. Your sons and daughters will prophesy, your young men will see visions, your old men will dream dreams.
>
> Even on my servants, both men and women, I will pour out my Spirit in those days, and they will prophesy.
>
> Acts 2:17-18 (NIV)

Visions

Kris Vallotton is Senior Associate Pastor at Bethel Church in Redding, California, and leads the School of Supernatural Ministry with his wife, Kathy. He tells us that he often sees visions. When prophesying encouragement and destiny over people at conferences, or in church, he sometimes sees something like a movie film or ticker tape over someone's head. It usually tells about something in that person's experience that will help confirm God's word for them. In his book, *Basic Training for Prophetic Ministry*, Vallotton explains a time when God showed him what was happening in a troubled young man's life.

Many years ago, I took a group of about 37 kids from our youth group to Santa Cruz, California, for a day on the beach. Among them was our foster daughter, Dee. It happened to be "Muscle Beach Day" and the area was overflowing with people. Our group found a spot to settle and enjoy the day.

Not long after our arrival, I glanced up and saw Dee running along the beach being chased by a man dressed in full leathers. As they ran toward us, I could hear the man shouting to Dee, "I love you! I love you! I'm taking you with me."

She ran to me for protection with this man close behind her. As she knelt next to me in the sand, he reached over and grabbed her by the blouse. He began to shake her, saying loudly, "I love you! I love you!"

Finally, I mustered the courage to grab the man's arm. "That's enough!" I yelled. The man abruptly dropped Dee in the sand, then turned and grabbed me, lifting me up off my knees! He screamed at me, "I love her! I'm taking her with me!"

Just then I saw an open vision appear above his head. Events of his life flashed over him in what appeared to be short video clips! I said to him, "Your mother is in the hospital dying, isn't she?"

"Yes!" he exclaimed.

"Your dad died last year, didn't he?" I shouted.

"Yeah," he said.

Then I yelled, "And you blame yourself, don't you?"

With a look of shock and disbelief he said, "Man, you're scaring me!" He turned around and ran away.

I jumped to my feet and chased after him! The whole event turned into quite a scene for the other beachgoers as I caught up with him and tackled him three times. Each time I tackled him, I yelled "YOU NEED JESUS!"

"I know!" he yelled back.

The outrageous event ended when he turned and ran toward his motorcycle gang. He stopped about a hundred yards from me, turned and shouted, "You pray for me!"

"What's your name?"

He shouted back, "Phillip."

The Bible

God speaks through His Bible, which those who follow Christ understand and believe to be the inspired message of God to His human creation.

Whatever my circumstances in life, He always leads me—or has a friend lead me—to a verse, a parable, a poem, or a story in the Bible that speaks right into my situation. I have many favorite verses, and I continue to collect them, highlight them, and share them.

Have you ever been reading and something just jumps out? It may be taken out of the context of the verse, but I believe God speaks however He wants to in order to get my attention. The Bible truly is a living Word.

One day, I was worried about my lovely, risk-taking, smart, and sometimes over-trusting daughter. I prayed and prayed, knowing God loves her even more than I do and yet having a really hard time letting Him have her. I was reading Psalm 46, and the words jumped straight from the page and into my spirit.

> God is within her, she will not fall; God will help her at break of day.
>
> Psalm 46:5 (NIV)

I claimed that as a promise from God for my daughter. God's promises over her are promises to me, too. I have learned to trust in His plan for her and trust in His protection over her. My job is to love her, to encourage her, to call out the gold in her, and to always be there for her.

Verses are highlighted all over my Bible for different times in my life when I heard from God regarding a tough decision, difficulties in a job, sickness in the family, and times of stress, anxiety, and weakness. Today, those highlighted verses remind me of God's goodness, the love of Jesus, and the presence of the Holy Spirit. They help me remember that God has promised to prosper me, He desires to be with me, He loves me, and He is happy with me.

It's His book, written for His beloved children, the bride of His passion, His Church.

Through it we learn of His nature, His love, and His purposes.

Signs

One of the signs I see a lot is triple numbers on digital clocks and license plates.

There was a season when seeing these brought much comfort. It was a difficult time in my husband's and my life together—a perfect storm of business and financial disaster that took its toll on us mentally and emotionally.

Waking up frequently at all hours of the night was common for us then. What was remarkable was we both would always wake up right at 1:11 a.m., 2:22 a.m., 3:33 a.m., 4:44 a.m., or 5:55 a.m. Did I mention we weren't together when these signs happened? Rick was working a job three hours away and living in an onsite dorm called a "man camp" located on a natural gas field.

This happened for months, and we knew it was from God, even if we didn't know what it meant. We later learned numbers have meaning. Triple numbers have more meaning. When we went to a Christian conference during that time, a woman told us she felt that the numbers meant "things are lining up, and the time is now."

During that season, I also liked to just think of the comfort I felt knowing God was with me every night. He knew what we were going through. He heard our prayers. The signs made me feel safe.

Dreams

There are so many books on dream interpretation. Suffice it to say that our dreams really are a way to hear from God. Sometimes He speaks directly through dreams, and sometimes He speaks in metaphors. Write your dreams down then check resources, and ask God to help you. See if you can learn to interpret what He may be saying through them. Joseph and Daniel in the Bible interpreted others' dreams from God. This brought them before rulers and propelled them into their destiny. Where could your dreams be taking you?

Words of Knowledge

Our church conducted a special service where guest speakers imparted joy, laughter, and hope into many whom had never heard that kind of message in the church. After the service, my friend DB went forward for healing prayer for her foot and ankle. While she was moving forward, my young friend Sarah called out, asking if anyone needed prayer for an ankle. God had given Sarah what is called a "word of knowledge." DB responded, and I joined Sarah and one of the speakers in prayer for my friend. While praying, I noticed her toe ring then saw in the Spirit a glowing circle of light whirling around her ankle and foot. DB said she felt heat. The following day, she called to tell me she was completely healed. It is now a year later, and she is still pain free.

These are just a few of the ways we can hear from God. Spend some time in prayer and find out how He is speaking to you. Sometimes he'll change his strategies and communicate in different ways. Be open. Listen. Trust that He is speaking. Write down what you believe He is saying.

How Does God Hear From Us?

God wants us to talk to Him through prayer. But where is He? How does He hear us? What about when we don't make sense to ourselves let alone Him?

When my grandson Trey was two years old, he was very, very sick with a virus. He would lay limp in his mommy's arms, eyes glazed over, and pale as could be. He was like that for a few days, not eating and not playing. The day the fever broke, we all celebrated with joy when he wanted to go outside to play in the fresh air. Our boy was back.

Two years later, Trey and his mom (my daughter Erin) were sitting on our porch talking about having gone to the doctor to get shots. "They poked your grandson," the little guy said as he looked at me with big, concerned eyes. Then he started talking about the time he had "beepers." Erin asked him what he meant. Again, he said "beepers." Remember, Mom? I was sick with beepers?" We started to chuckle, not understanding what he was talking about. He got more frustrated and tried to say it more loudly and more clearly. "*Beepers!*"

A few days later, Erin called to tell me, "*Fever.* He meant fever!" He had remembered that time two years ago when he was so sick. The loving mother knew it was important to her son for her to understand him. She didn't quit trying until she figured it out.

That's how our Father God is. The Holy Spirit has been given to us to take our prayers to God and to make it clear to Him even when we don't think we can say it clearly or don't even know how to pray. Our spirit speaks to His Spirit.

He always hears and always understands, and there is always an answer.

Thankfulness

I am sitting at Big Shooters Coffee Shop on Park Avenue in Kremmling. A grandpa and grandma are watching their little granddaughter eat her ice cream and open a great big birthday gift. She pulls out a beautiful music box, a carousel horse. Her grandpa winds it, and it plays a pretty tune. "Thank you!" she squeals. She names the horse Cinderella and says she will play it when she goes to sleep. Her delight is genuine. Her face shines with joy. "I like it," she says. Grandpa and Grandma beam. She has thanked them three times in the last few minutes. "Thank you for buying this for me. I love it," she says again.

That's how God is. He delights in giving us good gifts. He is so attracted to our delight and thankfulness when we love what He gives us. I believe it makes Him want to give us more gifts.

What if the little girl had sulked? What if she hadn't wanted to open the gift so lovingly selected and wrapped for her? What if she had wanted something different and didn't care what was in the box? Worse yet, what if she had opened it and thrown it to the side, unhappy? How would her grandparents have felt? Would they be eager to give her more presents?

I'm thinking (and I speak as a grandma) that I wouldn't be compelled to give her gifts very often. And

I wouldn't delight in selecting that something special because my experience would say she wouldn't appreciate it.

God has so many gifts for us. He longs for us to hunger and desire and anticipate what He wants to give us. He leaves clues and messages for us and stands by, waiting for us to notice. How long are we going to ignore Him? How long are we going to reject His gifts? How long are we going to complain that He hasn't answered all of our prayers or hasn't given us all we want?

God is attracted—just like a loving grandparent and parent—to our appreciation and thankfulness. One huge thing I have discovered as I learn His nature and how much He loves me is that I, in my love and honor for Him, want to be thankful for what He has done and is doing and will do. I refuse to be worried, complaining, or regretful about what He hasn't done yet.

When He blesses us, we should always thank Him, and only then do we have permission to ask for more.

We are made in His image. If we delight in giving gifts to our appreciative children, how much more does our Father in heaven delight in giving gifts to us?

> If you then, though you are evil, know how to give good gifts to your children, how much more will your Father in heaven give the Holy Spirit to those who ask him!
>
> Luke 11:13 (NIV)

> Every good and perfect gift is from above, coming down from the Father of heavenly lights, who does not change like shifting shadows.
>
> James 1:17 (NIV)

God created man to be in relationship with Him. It's not about us just praying. It's also about us listening. Conversation is a two-way dialogue. We must learn to listen to the voice of a loving and wise Father, who guides us and helps us navigate our lives until we reach the hope and future he has promised. (See Jeremiah 29:11.)

So who *is* this One who wants to talk to us?

A Blessing for You

I bless you with understanding how God talks to you and how He hears from you. May you discover how thankfulness works and experience what happens in your life when you remember and are grateful for what God is doing, happily expectant of future answers to your prayers. I pray you will have such experience with God that you can teach others that they, too, can hear Him through:

Still, small voice—like a clear whisper in your ear or mind.

Audible voice.

Thoughts—creative ideas and directions you wouldn't normally think of.

Images—pictures and colors you imagine. These may mean something for you or someone else.

Visions—in dreams or awake. God will show you what He wants you to know.

The Bible—Powerful revelation from God's living word.

Signs—Coincidences, or repetitions that catch your attention.

Dreams—Sleep time is when God has our undivided attention. Write them down!

Words of Knowledge—Often these are impressions, body pains, or words of wisdom God is giving you to help someone else.

There are many more ways God can speak to you. Ask Him to show you.

Reflect and Receive

1. How does God speak to you? How would you like Him to speak to you?
2. What are you thankful for?
3. What are you praying in thankful expectation for?
4. Make these declarations daily over yourself: "I am thankful. I don't worry. I trust God."
5. Watch for what God is doing and testify to others when He answers your prayers.

The Design and Designer

...I have put wisdom in the hearts of all the
gifted artisans, that they may make all that I
have commanded you...

Exodus 30:34 (NKJV).

How Long Are You Going to Live?

One summer day I was driving home with my small
grandson Trey after his T-ball game. I gave him my
wallet to hold while I buckled him into his car seat. My
driver's license was tucked into a window on the front
of the wallet, and he studied it carefully. I let him keep
it while we drove.

"Is this *you*, Grandma?"

"Yes."

"You look so smooth," he complimented. Then came the bubble burst. "And *now* you have lines! How long are you gonna live?"

In all of his five-year-old innocence, he was asking the deep things. Between the "lines" I could hear him wondering about life.

I told him I had lines because I'm a grandma. He figured that as soon as my hair turned white, I'd go to heaven. I didn't have the heart to tell him it's not really the color he thinks it is now.

It didn't stop there. He wanted to be sure his whole family would be together in heaven.

Jesus also wanted this. Speaking to His disciples and down the centuries to all of His children on the night He was betrayed, He assured us He is with us. I picture Him looking at His friends, compassion overflowing in His heart for what they were about to go through on His account. He assures them, and He assures us:

> I will not leave you as orphans; I will come to you. Before long, the world will not see me anymore, but you will see me. Because I live, you also will live. On that day you will realize that I am in my Father, and you are in me, and I am in you.
>
> John 14:18-20 (NIV)

And then Jesus, the beloved Son, prays to His Father, the Creator of the universe:

> Father, I want those you have given me to be
> with me where I am, and to see my glory, the
> glory you have given me because you loved me
> before the creation of the world.

John 17: 24 9 (NIV)

And He says to his friends down through the generations:

> I go and prepare a place for you, I will come
> back and take you to be with me that you also
> may be where I am.

John 14:3 (NIV)

Let Go!

> From the ends of the earth I call to you, I call as
> my heart grows faint; lead me to the rock that
> is higher than I.

Psalm 61:2 (NIV)

My daughter Erin always surprises me. As a child she was quiet, feminine (still is), and always sure of herself. It was amazing to see her wrestle piglets, get dirty, and love every moment of her 4-H livestock experiences.

In college, she worked for a guest ranch in Wyoming that also raised an array of ranch and exotic animals, including camels. One day, she was helping wrangle a steer—something she had not had prior experience with.

She was on foot and led the critter with a rope. Suddenly, it bolted. Surprised, she began to run after it, then fell, still hanging onto the rope. The steer dragged her for some distance across the rocky and sage-covered terrain before she heard the cries of her coworkers to "Let go!" She did, and painful bruises and abrasions from the ordeal took months to heal.

Should You Let Go?

Sometimes life does that to us, doesn't it? We hang on, trying to make something work. Trying every solution. Not giving up. Some people call it "beating a dead horse." We just know we can do it if we just don't give up. We refuse to stop trying. Our last penny is thrown at the problem. We have painful abrasions. Only then do we come in a desperate cry before our God.

"Help! What should I do?"

God in His wonderful love and grace is always present to meet us. He gathers us up in His arms. He gently pries our fingers loose and gives us the wisdom we have asked for.

"Let go!" He urges.

"But I can't. Everything will fall. I don't want to fail. I'm afraid. I can't let go."

"Let go, and see what I can do."

A few years ago, Rick and I were at that point. With every log home we built, we would say this is the one that will put us ahead. But it seemed that with each new project, it became more difficult to make ends meet.

Finally, in 2008, we took a financial risk to bring our log home construction business to a new level. That same year, the big recession and housing downturn brought the walls caving in. Every morning I woke up worried about Rick and the stress he was under. I worried about the bills, the loans, and everything I could think of that "deserved" worry. Our savings dwindled as we tried to keep our guys paid and the business above water. And then one cold fall day, after talking with another creditor who refused to help us, something inside of me said *enough*.

We had to let go. We had to stop the downward spiral. *What's the worst that can happen?* I thought. *Well, we could lose our business, which had been our dream. We may lose our home. We would probably have to file for bankruptcy. We would lose our good credit standing.*

But we might have peace. We could start over. My husband's life might be healthier. At that point the unknown felt better than the known. We swallowed our pride and made an appointment with a lawyer.

All the things I feared happened. In one tumultuous season, after much wise counsel and prayer, we filed for bankruptcy, foreclosed on our home, closed our business, and started over.

One day, a few months after all that happened, I was meeting with a group of friends who gathered regularly to learn how to hear from God. We would pray, listen, write notes, and discuss what we thought God was saying and doing. During worship, while just being quiet with the music, I saw a vision, or perhaps it was a dream. The back of one of my legs had a deep, dark, open wound. Out of the wound, green plants were sprouting. It seemed like I had no idea that I was injured, hurting, or even aware of the gash. Then I woke up. Looking back now, I feel like it was a promise from

God of Romans 8:28: "And we know that in all things God works for the good of those who love him, who have been called according to his purpose."

There was good that was going to come out of the pain. This would all soon be behind me, and I would not feel the hurt and desperation any longer.

I would never advise anyone to suffer the route we went through. Bankruptcy, foreclosure, and starting over are extreme and not the solutions for everyone. The answers to your problems are indeed a matter between you and God, and I urge you to pray and seek.

My question, however, is: Are you desperately holding on to something that it is time to release? It could be a business matter, a relationship, a dream, a financial issue, or a health matter. Have you asked yourself what might happen if you let go? Are you hearing a still, small voice, a whisper, or a message from your Creator who made you and knows everything about you? Are you hearing "let go?"

God says in His Word to ask Him for wisdom, and He freely gives it. He'll give you ideas, creativity, words to say, and a sense of timing. He also gives Himself.

When we "let go," we put into motion an amazing sequence of wisdom, divine appointments, divine health, divine provision, peace, and, yes, even joy. God's strategies working with us are much stronger than us trying to tell God how we want things to happen. God's wisdom is higher than our wisdom. His love is greater than our love. When we let go, we open a way for Him to meet our needs His way. It's the most exciting of adventures.

"For my thoughts are not your thoughts, neither are your ways my ways," declares the Lord. "As the heavens are higher than the earth, so are my ways higher than your ways and my thoughts than your thoughts."

Isaiah 55:8-9 (NIV)

My goal is that they may be encouraged in heart and united in love, so that they may have the full riches of complete understanding, in order that they may know the mystery of God, namely, Christ, in whom are hidden all the treasures of wisdom and knowledge.

Colossians 2:2-3 (NIV)

When we trust Him with everything, we enter into a new reality of discovering our gifts, our purpose, our calling, and our dreams.

Please, please, please don't go through life without Him. We have much to do.

And with the Master Designer, it is all good.

Do you know who He is now? There are so many facets to His character. Your Designer—the person who fashioned your very life—is loving, kind, and good. He's *for* you. He stands cheering at the sidelines for you. He helps you when you call on Him and when you don't. His plans for you are better than your plans for yourself.

Take His hand. Let Him guide you. Ask Him if you need to let go of something.

His heart is to be with you always, to be where you are now, and to be in heaven with you for eternity.

Will you follow His lead? Will you get to know the Holy Spirit whom Jesus gave you to help you scale the heights and plumb the depths of your life?

It's time to get into the river and flow with the life He has for you.

A Blessing for You

I bless you as you take these five steps to finding freedom in your life:

1. Let go.
2. Trust God. You are not alone. Learn His promises. He will never leave you or forsake you.
3. Receive peace. When anxiety, worry, fear, and stress come, give them to God and take from Him His peace that passes understanding.
4. Move forward. Ask your loving heavenly Papa about the new steps ahead.
5. Be thankful. Determine to have a grateful heart for what He is doing now, and joyful hope for what is ahead.

> Now to Him who is able to do exceedingly abundantly above all that we ask or think, according to the power that works in us, to Him be the glory in the church by Christ Jesus to all generations, forever and ever. Amen.
>
> Ephesians 3:20-21 (NKJV)

Reflect and Receive

1. What will you be letting go of? What could set you free if you gave it to God?

2. Imagine your life free from this one thing. What could your life look like? Think about your creativity, your dreams, and your relationships. How would they be different?

3. If you are not sure about any of this, ask God to make you aware of anything that might be holding you back from what He has created you to be and to do. Read James 1:5 and ask for wisdom.

4. Name two strategies you could accomplish this week as you begin to loosen your control over circumstances you feel God wants you to let go of.

River Dance

The Rapids

There is a river whose streams make glad the city of God.

Psalm 46:4 (NIV)

When we float in a river, we realize we are subject to nature's power and energy. If we flow with the current, it is pleasant, freeing, and peaceful. If we fight against the current, we find quickly that we lose ground and get nowhere fast.

There are universal laws about rivers and currents. In my younger years, I was a raft captain for activities at Idlewild Guest Ranch. We took guests down the beautiful Little Gore Canyon of the Colorado River from the put-in point at a beach called The Pumphouse to the beach at the riverside town of Radium. Normally the river was easy to navigate, taking us through beautiful red rock canyons. The sunny days and cold water were exhilarating. If someone fell overboard, it was easy to bring them back on board if they didn't panic.

There is one stretch of the river called Needle's Eye, where the river flows between two large rocks that are sometimes right under the surface when the river is high. I had to learn to read the river to know just when to paddle strong and position the raft to flow in between the hidden rocks.

Rafts that didn't maneuver correctly would get stuck on a rock or tip precariously in the rushing waters. I have to say I lost a few guests in that stretch, but all happily survived.

God's river in the Bible is a metaphor for the Holy Spirit. The river is beautifully gentle when we enter in, trusting the Holy Spirit with the events and challenges we are facing. In the deeper water, He carries us in His powerful arms. In the rougher waters, He remains with us and leads us to safety. And if we trust Him, we can actually have fun in the danger zones, curiously anticipating what He will do. If, in some areas of life, we get scared, we are at those times moving against the river's current, and we limit what God is able to do in our lives. When we think we can navigate without Him, that's when we get hung up in the shallows and shipwrecked on the shore.

Are you ready to stay in the river with God and allow the Holy Spirit to tell you when to paddle and when not to? Are you ready to trust the Master Captain with your life and all you care about?

Flowing with the river is easy. It's about what Jesus said when He promised:

> Come to me all you who are weary and bur-
> dened, and I will give you rest. Take my yoke
> upon you and learn from me, for I am gentle
> and humble in heart, and you will find rest for
> your souls. For my yoke is easy, and my burden
> is light.
>
> Matthew 11:28-30 (NIV)

We Are a Current Flowing With His Gifts

I stood watching the worship leader at a Sunday night Bethel Church service. This man has written songs I've sung for years, and he was now about twenty feet from me. He was singing to a big crowd and worshiping with all he had in him. "Hallelujah, to the God of the redeemed," he sang, and the presence of the Lord fell upon the gathering of saints.

Then he dropped to his knees, guitar hanging from his neck, and he raised his hands as the band played and the crowd continued to sing. Sweat pouring from his forehead and tears streaming from his eyes, he was immersed in his own praises to his Father. As I watched him use every gift he'd been given to worship in purity, love, and humility, he led me right to the One who deserves my praise.

How can we use our own gifts to worship God?

He is the Giver of our gifts. When we use them and give them away to others, we bring praise and honor to our Father in heaven.

Are you a writer, a songwriter, a musician, or an artist? Do you have creative ideas for business? Are you an inventor, a culinary artist, or do you have a way with wood or cloth or flowers? We are made in His image. He is the first and the ultimate Creator of everything—including us. He has put a facet of the same creativity He possesses into each one of us.

Like the worship leader, we each have an amazing opportunity to lead others into the purist of praises to our King by using and sharing the creative gifts He has given us.

In this atmosphere of worship, God is present in our midst.

> But you are holy, enthroned in the praises of
> Israel.
>
> Psalms 22:3 (NKJV)

The Bible says God is enthroned in the praises of His people. Another translation says He inhabits our praises. When we praise Him with song or by using our gifts, He is among us.

Knowing this, how can we help but fall to our knees at His feet? How can we resist calling His name? How can we not sense His power and presence among us? How can we even have time to worry about what others think?

How I want to be like that worship leader—giving my all in praise to the Father—not only through song, and not just in prayer, but in giving back to Him *who* He created me to be.

Will you pray this prayer with me?

> God, help me to worship you with my gifts without being shy, embarrassed, worrying about others around me, or feeling unworthy. I shall not fear man any longer. I am worthy to share my gifts because You make me worthy. Like David, I want to worship you in abandonment—my King, my God, my Redeemer, and my Friend. Amen.

> Oh yes, I'll dance to God's glory—more recklessly even than this. And as far as I'm concerned, I'll gladly look like a fool.
>
> 2 Samuel 6:20-22 (The Message)

Let the King of Glory Enter In

Not long ago, I found myself stressed out, anxious, striving, and irritated for no real reason. I stumbled and crashed, and soon, marching across my Bible, came the Psalms. God was showing me in His gentle way that I had left Him out of several days.

How do we leave Him out? Don't we carry Him with us always? Well, yes and no. It's more like He carries us in His love and joy over us, even when we're forgetting Him.

I had put up a wall without knowing it. It was a wall of "I can do this myself," and, "I'm so tired. I'll spend time with God tomorrow."

A wonderful truth is: He enjoys my company, and he surrounds me with Himself. If I don't hear Him talking or sense Him near me, it's not Him; it's me listening to something other than His voice.

What other walls keep us from Him? Well, there's fear, hopelessness, addictions, and false beliefs about God to name a few. Or it can be more subtle, like laziness, offense, unforgiveness, or busyness.

Psalm 24 tells us it's time to let the King of glory enter in (into my day, my soul, my mind, my home, my work, my family, my love, my waking, and my sleeping) with all His majesty, glory, and power.

> He who has clean hands and a pure heart, who does not lift up his soul to an idol or swear by what is false, he will receive blessing from the Lord and vindication from God his Savior. Such is the generation of those who seek Him, who seek your face, O God of Jacob. Lift up your heads, O you gates; lift them up, you ancient doors, that the King of glory may come in. Who is he, this King of glory? The Lord Almighty—he is the King of Glory!
>
> Psalms 24 (NIV)

Jump in the River

A few years ago, before we attended ministry school and while we were going through our financial breakdown, I spent a lot of time praying during sleepless nights and confusing days. One clear message I kept hearing from God in my thoughts was: *Stay in the river.*

What did that mean? I started to look up verses about the river and read what others said about it. For me, it became a message of security. If I stayed in the river and flowed with the current at the pace God was moving—not ahead or behind—I would be okay. On days when I forgot to pray and got too busy, I would tend to feel scared and agitated. Then I would hear in my spirit, *Get back in the river.* At those times, I realized that in my agitation, I had climbed into the tangled bushes on the riverbanks and gotten stuck. So, I would rest in Him for a few moments and imagine myself getting back in the river. It always brought refreshing restoration and peace.

As we discussed a few pages ago, references to water and river in the Bible many times refer to the Holy Spirit.

Even though it's clear in the Bible that He is an equal third of the Trinity, the Holy Spirit has in modern times been largely ignored. This is called "cessationism" meaning the Holy Spirit's power as defined by such gifts of the Spirit as healing, speaking in tongues, and prophecy was just meant for the early church, and is not for today.

I had this belief most of my life. It was part of my fear of joining the Jesus Movement—too radical. I used to like the safety of Sunday morning church and the tradition of holy services, bowed heads, and organized worship.

And then I didn't.

It wasn't long after I went to college that these practices did not hold me at all. My heart hungered for more. My spirit yearned to know a purpose in life to live for. It took me a long time to find it.

In the past ten years, I have learned for myself that Holy Spirit is alive and well, and working with God and Son to give us a purpose, a hope, and a plan right here, right now, before our physical bodies die.

Jesus promised to send the Helper, the Holy Spirit, to us to help us and instruct us. It's the Holy Spirit—God's Spirit—that talks to us, gives us ideas, urges us on, and encourages us.

We have the mind of Christ—a supernatural wisdom and creativity revealed to us by the Holy Spirit—for the purpose of living an abundant life, carrying out the plans of the Savior. Through the Holy Spirit, we have authority and power to destroy the works of the enemy and bring glory to God. We are called to partner with God, Jesus, and Holy Spirit in advancing the kingdom of God on earth.

I hear you saying, "How can I know this for sure?"

Do you have a Bible in a translation that is easy for you to understand? I like my New International Version. The Message Bible offers a paraphrased narrative that is more like today's language. Many of my friends like the New King James Version. There are other translations, too. Find one you like and read it. It's not hard to understand the Bible if you ask God to help you.

I want to direct you to two books in God's Scriptures that will help you discover the Holy Spirit for yourself.

The first one is the book of the Gospel of John. It is all about Jesus, written by a man who was His friend, one of the disciples, and an eyewitness to all that happened during Jesus's three years of ministry as a man.

The Book of John

John was there when Jesus was crucified. He was among those saddened, desperate, and fearful as to what was happening. From the cross, Jesus asked John to take care of Mary, His mother. John felt like he was Jesus's best friend and the most loved. He watched as Jesus took His final breath, and the sky darkened, the earth rumbled, and the curtain of the temple tore in half.

And then the unimaginable happened. John writes that Jesus was raised from the dead. He lived and walked among the people for forty days before he ascended to the Father in heaven. He spoke with them, fished with them, made them breakfast on the beach of the Sea of Galilee, instructed them, loved them, and made them many promises. When He ascended to heaven, it was after He asked them to wait.

> Do not leave Jerusalem, but wait for the gift my Father promised, which you have heard me speak about. For John baptized with water, but in a few days you will be baptized with the Holy Spirit.
>
> Acts 1:4 (NIV)

Wait For What?

Jesus asked them to wait for the Helper that He would send. He wanted them to wait in Jerusalem until the Helper came. It was a gift to them—and to all that would believe in His name—to empower them to do the works He asked them, and us, to do.

That brings us to the other book I'd like you to know about. In the book of Acts, the story continues.

The Book of Acts

Acts is written by Luke, an associate of Paul, who wrote from eyewitness accounts of Jesus's life, resurrection, and the birth of the Church. In Acts, Luke tells of the people in the Upper Room—the ones who waited as the Lord had asked. They waited day and night for the promised gift, believing in faith. Then, after many days, in one amazing moment, a *whoosh* of wind came into the room, and flames of fire rested on each person. It was an imparting of the promised Holy Spirit. Proof of the empowering Spirit happened the following morning.

The ones who had been in the Upper Room were filled with boldness. Peter, who just days ago out of fear for his life had denied he knew Jesus, now spoke with authority. He taught about Jesus with demonstrations of supernatural power. The Upper Room members spoke in different languages as the Spirit enabled them so that all who were in the city for the Day of

Pentecost would receive the news of the living Christ in their native language. Three thousand gave their lives to Christ at that first meeting; and in the days to come, as the disciples carried the word out to others, thousands more believed.

Signs and Wonders

The book of Acts has many accounts of the disciples using signs and wonders to draw the attention and desire of the people to the Lord. The blind, deaf, and lame were healed. The crowds were amazed. Then when Peter was persecuted and thrown into prison, an angel miraculously came and released him. These are just a few accounts. There are so many in Acts.

John concludes his gospel saying that if all the stories were told of all the things that Jesus did, "the world would not have room for the books that would be written."

Filled with the Spirit

Many of the accounts of miracles say that the disciples were "filled with the Spirit" before miracles would happen.

Jesus gives us the Holy Spirit in the same way that He breathed on His disciples after His resurrection. (See John 20:22.)

> Again Jesus said, "Peace be with you! As the Father has sent me, I am sending you." And with

> that he breathed on them and said, "Receive the
> Holy Spirit. If you forgive anyone's sins, their
> sins are forgiven; if you do not forgive them,
> they are not forgiven."

John 20:21-23 (NIV)

The Spirit not only instructs us and helps us to find the truth in Scripture and discern the truth in our lives, but He also empowers us and gives us authority to represent King Jesus on earth.

In the same chapter, in a meeting with the disciples a week later, the resurrected Jesus tells His disciple, Thomas:

> Because you have seen me, you have believed;
> blessed are those who have not seen and yet
> have believed.

John 20:29 (NIV)

Can you see yourself in this? His words are for the disciples *and* for us—all who believe.

What Is This Baptism of the Holy Spirit?

John the Baptist baptized with water. He was to herald the coming of the Son of God. But after him would come One—Jesus Christ, the Son—who would baptize with the Holy Spirit and fire. (See John 1:29.)

There are *two* times Jesus addressed this receiving of the Holy Spirit. First, He breathed on his disciples and

said "receive." Later, He said to wait for the gift. It was a different experience. And it came with wind and fire, and it imparted power and wisdom.

So how do we enter into this gift? How do we know we have it? Can we simply ask God for it?

Yes. Ask God to give it to you. If you have already received it, ask Him for more.

Let me help you:

> Lord, I pray for my friends reading this book, and we thank You that You are real and alive and present in our midst. We thank You for Your desires for us and that You want to relate to us as Your sons and daughters. We love it that You call us friends. We want to live out Your Word and fulfill Your purposes in our lives. We ask for wisdom and strength. Please fill us with Your Spirit. Holy Spirit, come!

God will answer this prayer. How will you know?

You will sense it. You may have a physical manifestation. Some people feel tingling or electricity. You may feel nothing at all. It's all okay. You are okay. Just know that God is always faithful to answer our prayers, and He is indeed doing something in you right now.

Prayer Language

Some people, when receiving the Holy Spirit, begin to speak in another language—a spiritual tongue. This is called a prayer language, and you can ask God for this gift. You may receive it right away, or it may come later.

Be open to it. Ask someone who has a prayer language to pray with you to receive it. It is for your strengthening and for God's glory when we use it. And please do not feel left out if you don't have it now. God is going to bless your socks off in so many ways. It will come if you want it. I promise.

Presence of the Holy Spirit

In worship, you may sense His presence resting on you. Sometimes it may feel so heavy that you want to kneel down. Some people weep. Others laugh. Trust that these are all experiences in God. He loves to relate to us in many surprising ways. Please give space for this in yourself and for those around you. Like David in his wild dancing before the Lord, we must overcome embarrassment or worries of the judgment of others. This is your Maker. He is worthy of our bodies, souls, and spirits expressing themselves in worship.

Be Filled!

We can be filled again and again as we give ourselves over to the purposes we were made for.

When you worship, ask Him to fill you with more of Himself. When you pray for others, understand His presence is with you and you are imparting to them the Spirit of God. When you minister and give of yourself to the sick and hopeless, He promises to fill you more. Pray for it. He will answer you with Himself.

Righteousness, Peace, and Joy

> For the kingdom of God is not a matter of eating and drinking, but of righteousness, peace and joy in the Holy Spirit.
>
> Romans 14:17 (NIV)

We are righteous because Jesus Christ found us worthy and paid the ransom for our souls. God loves us. He wants us to walk in the glory of His kingdom. Like a loving Father, He wants us to understand we are legally adopted and have full rights and access to all the resources of heaven—the same as His Son, Jesus Christ.

We are royalty—sons and daughters of God, coheirs with Christ the King, princesses and princes, kings and queens. Amazingly, He considers us friends. What a wonderful Lord we have. Are we to continue to walk downtrodden, heads low, hearts crying for mercy and forgiveness, always remembering the past, our defeats, our problems, and our sin? No. *We are righteous and worthy because He is righteous and worthy*, and He paid a dear price for us.

So what do we do with that?

Will we stay at the foot of the cross, weeping in what we believe is humility? Or will we take up our cross, run through the meadow, and climb the hill into our destiny—the life He died for so that we could live it? True humility is recognizing the price He paid and living in full awareness of who He made us to be.

> Holy Spirit, come. Fill us. Give us wisdom. Help us to know what it means to have the

mind of Christ. Thank You for all you have done, Jesus. Help us to give You what You paid for; to walk in the purposes You called us to as Your sons and daughters.

We enter his peace. The kingdom of God is peace. When we live in the kingdom, we live as if we are seated in heaven at the feet of God the Father in the throne room. From that perspective of peace, authority, and power, we are able to see our situations on earth from God's position. Like Jesus, we can shout to any storm, darkness, worry, disease, or problem and say, "Peace, be still." With the authority given to us, His children, we can expect circumstances to bow at the name of Jesus. When we understand the power and greatness of the One we call our Father, Daddy, and Papa God, we trust Him to take care of us. We enter His peace.

A Third of the Kingdom Is Joy

Joy is mentioned so many times in God's Word. It's the kind of joy that is more than a passing smile or cheerful word. I believe it is dancing, laughing, tearful, hilarious joy—the kind that brings healing and energy and overcomes anything the enemy wants to hurl at us. The devil hates it when we laugh. Our joy is a mighty weapon. So laugh as much as you can. Laugh with me at ourselves, our situations, the hard things in our life. Laugh hysterically. If you can't drum it up, it's okay to act it out until hilarity takes over. I know you can do it. See how different life becomes when we live it in a kingdom of pure joy.

Created for a Purpose

We are created by a divine Maker. He does not make mistakes. He has put into us His DNA. He has distributed gifts to us to give to those He puts on our hearts. We cannot keep what we don't give away. When we receive our gifts—or recognize what skills and talents He has deposited into us—and use them for the benefit of others, we, in turn, are rewarded with great pleasure and joy.

The Gift Shop

How do you discover the creative gifts God has given you?

Is there something that you would do because you love to do it, even if it never makes money? Is there something that, when you are doing it, time passes without notice? Is there something that you do that, when you are finished, you have a sense of joy and accomplishment?

That quite possibly is the area God has gifted you in. I have a list of books and resources at the end of this book that will help you discover your gifts, your talents, and your calling.

This is real. And we have a Holy Spirit helper that partners with us every step of the way. God in three persons—championing us to reach the destiny He has lovingly created us for.

We have some choices to make. What is the most important work we can do for God?

Jesus said: "The work of God is this: to believe in the one He has sent" (John 6:29 NIV).

He is a good God, and He has a good life planned for you. Step ahead. No striving. No stress. Only believe. Watch for His signs. Listen for His voice.

You are beginning to know Him, the presence of His Holy Spirit, His character, His love, and His kindness.

Are you ready to trust Him as you step in the river? Are you ready to let go and let Him guide you in His gentle current?

How is the water?

Rest and flow as we learn to recognize God's golden thread through our life's experiences.

A Blessing for You

God not only planned what you would look like, but in His divine joy, he planned who you would be. You are unique from everyone else. I bless you to discover the joy of the kingdom, along with the righteousness and the peace. May joy be part of every thought, every moment, every plan and decision. I bless you to discover the purpose you were created for, as you discover the Comforter, the Holy Spirit, in a tangible, experiential way. Holy Spirit, I pray you would reveal right now the gifts that have been given to my friend.

Reflect and Receive

1. Name one purpose you feel you were created for. For example, without thinking of anyone else or

what they might think about you, answer the questions: Who are you? Why are you?

2. Make a list of what you enjoy doing. How can you discover your gifts and talents in that list?

3. What is unique about you, your personality, and your character?

The Golden Thread

> They hammered out thin sheets of gold and cut strands to be worked into the blue, purple and scarlet yarn and fine linen—the work of skilled hands.
>
> Exodus 39:3 (NIV)

Gold is written of throughout the Bible in many ways. It is a symbol of wealth. It is used to teach about investment. There are cautions and teachings over its misuse. In the desert travels of the Nation of Israel, it was used as a covering for vessels in the Tabernacle that contained incense, manna from heaven, and the very presence of God.

I use the Golden Thread here to illustrate something precious. It is the strand woven in and out of the tapestry of our own personal history of experiences with God. Its brilliance shines as we see God's hand in our lives and His character in those we love. It represents some of the high points of our life as we remember His blessings.

A closer look reveals some tarnished moments. Yet we can still see the gold, the evidence of His Holy Spirit in those times, too.

Hovering over the Dark Waters

In the Creation story in Genesis, the Holy Spirit is revealed as brooding over the dark waters like a bird. (See Genesis 1:2, The Message.)

The Holy Spirit is a messenger, the One who accomplishes the heart of the Father—the brooder and prayer. Holy Spirit broods over you and me, over our children, and those we pray for. We can ask the Holy Spirit through prayer to hover over our loved ones until God is formed in them. It is a powerful and effective prayer, and a prayer that God honors, for it is praying His will. Beni Johnson offers a commentary on this in her book, *The Happy Intercessor.*[1]

I have prayed this prayer every time I ask for God's guidance, protection, provision, and help for my children and grandchildren. I have seen His hand in circumstances I've prayed for. When I have written my prayers down in my journal and then gone back to them at a later time, I have been able to see the way God is answering them. Then I thank Him for answered prayers and pray for continued breakthrough.

It is good for us to be conscious and aware of answers to our prayers. In that way, we are able to follow the tapestry needle as it guides the golden fiber through our life. It is a wonderful and surprising revelation when we are aware of how God is handling a situation. He continues to amaze me as He proves time and again that His answers are always better than what I requested.

Beauty in Chaos

My Bible tends to be a catchall for the important things of life—like pictures, notes, church bulletins, papers, bookmarks, and things I always plan to read later.

On a recent morning, papers were falling out, the binding was feeling lopsided, and the leather cover was looking thirsty. For some time now, every time I grabbed my Bible, I thought, *Someday I need to do something about all of this.*

Today is the day!

I carefully remove the loose contents, and I'm propelled into a few special moments.

Like a treasure chest, my Bible is host to several cute family photos, revealing how my grandchildren have changed. How adorable and little they were as I tucked their photos inside a few years ago. I love discovering them among the pages and praying for them when I see them smiling out at me.

There are other pictures, too—one of a wild, pink rose that is so delicate and such a wonderful memory that I can almost smell its fragrance even now. I had taken several flower and scenery shots and made them into wallet-sized pictures to hand out to friends as an art project at ministry school. God would show me which photo to give to which person. I would write an encouraging word on the back about their destiny as God helped me to see the gold inside each one of them.

I find a little index card with a picture drawn of a battle. On the back is a little boy's wild handwriting, complete with illustrations, declaring over me that I was "born to defeat the trickery of the devil." This reminds me of a special day when children visited our monthly volunteer pastor meeting to give us words of prophecy. These young ones were learning to declare God's goodness and promises as part of their normal school curriculum.

Soon, I find a folded article about the significance of scientific truth as it relates to spiritual truth in regard to chronos time. My friend, Paula, shared it with me.

The most recent additions are three photos—two of the Eagles Nest mountain range in Colorado and one of my daughter, Bess, at age twelve (she's now twenty-five). A friend recently gave these prints to me, knowing I would love them.

Now, I'm looking at a quickly scrawled map of our new neighborhood in Parachute, Colorado, given to us by our landlord. He thoughtfully wrote the names of our neighbors and indicated where they lived around our court. I decide I will get out to meet them soon.

A bookmark that I never knew was in there reveals itself, showing a man on a bicycle, riding across a desert, with hands free of the handlebars and raised in victory. It reads: "Convergence: Integrating your Career, Community, Creativity, and Calling." My thoughts zoom back to the class that taught on this last year, and I reflect a few moments about how I am doing with all that I learned.

I reread the beautiful Mother's Day card made for me last year by Bess. It touched me so deeply when I received it that I just had to keep it in my Bible.

A folded paper with declarations of joy reminds me to daily come before my Father in praise and thankfulness, remembering all He is and has done in my life and declaring once more His promises over me. Here are a few:

> A merry heart is good medicine. I "take" this prescription of joy and laughter daily. As I do, my health and vitality are strengthened.
>
> I love God's ways. I build my life on the rock of God's Word. I obey God, and my joy is full as a result.
>
> I delight in what God is doing rather than dwell on what the devil says He is not doing. I daily hear the sound of His moving, and I respond with great delight and joy.
>
> (Thanks to Steve and Wendy Backlund for your teaching on declarations. Check the back of this book for more. Saying these every day can keep life in perspective.)

One of the oldest things in my Bible is a clipping from the *Sky-Hi News* in Granby, Colorado. It's a photo of our Grand County newspaper ski team at the annual

Press Cup at Winter Park Ski Area in 1980. I barely recognize my skinny self, posed with three other editors and reporters, race bibs and all.

A crisp ten-dollar bill and a one-dollar bill are the oldest of the treasures. I keep those in there to remind me of a time when I was a ski instructor in the 70s at Ski Idlewild Ski Area in Winter Park, Colorado. These bills were tips mailed to me by families with letters telling me how much they loved their lessons and their vacation. A ten-dollar tip in 1975 was a very big deal. I happened to discover them five years ago (thirty years later) while rummaging through old boxes.

A small, laminated picture of happy grandchildren bookmarks a special page in my Bible. The back of it reads: "Children's children are a crown to the aged, and parents are the pride of their children" (Proverbs 17:6).

I've used a list of four dreams written on half an index card as another bookmark since last summer, when my small group (we call ourselves the See More Sisters) wrote our dreams down during a meeting on a beautiful flowered deck with a view of the mountains.

My card reads:

1) Write three books by 2012.
2) Speak at a huge conference to encourage destiny and creativity.
3) Travel to five more countries by 2012.
4) Take all the grandkids and their parents on a trip.

I remember that my friend Cindy shared her long-time dream of owning a light-blue Volkswagen convertible. Fun! Our assignment was to pray over each other's dreams and see what God would do. Stay tuned…

Now I find a photo of me with daughter Erin that is like one of those mother/daughter look-alikes.

Ink lines and dots cascade across another piece of inkjet paper, drawn on a summer day I was playing with my eighteen-month-old granddaughter who was writing very important things for me.

Another treasure is a beautiful, hand-painted card filled with encouraging words and prophetic declarations for my husband and me; it's a reminder of a special time during a meeting last year at a Northern California bed and breakfast.

And finally, here is a paper I almost forgot about. When I first looked at it, I couldn't understand the message or figure out who wrote it. And then it clicked. It was written during a special session Rick and I had with a mentor who was giving us hope and business ideas for our "prosperous" future.

Looking at this pile before me, it is no wonder my Bible's binding is awry. The book that held these treasures now sits on the counter, absorbing a layer of olive oil I gently rubbed into the leather.

I like my Bible. It matches me: pages torn, binding bent, well used, and full of memories.

Sometimes I think my life has had little organization, and I see that as not a good thing. But today, in this exercise with my Bible, I see something more important than organization. I see life, messy as it is, pouring forth among relationships and words of kindness, a pattern of loveliness born from joy and sorrow, spontaneity and very little discipline.

Would I have it any other way?

I think not.

Do you see the gold?

Let me ask you, now. Are you seeing some of the golden threads in your life? As I look on the tapestry of my own life, I can see the golden theme from the beginning—through family times, vacations, accidents, hardships, broken hearts, happy births, lost loved ones, victories, and defeats. Sometimes the gold is bright, and it shines. Other times it is hard to detect a glimmer, and I have to look more closely. But if I try, I do indeed see its continuous flow through the times of my life.

A Blessing for You

I bless you to see with clarity God's woven presence in your life since childhood. I bless you to detect Him in the hard times and the good times; in relationships; in the white hair of old ones and the smile of a baby. I bless you to discover His golden thread woven through chaotic times when your thoughts were far from Him, as well as in peaceful times when things seemed to be going just fine.

Reflect and Receive

1. What have been some chaotic times in your life? How did you feel in those times?

2. What truths have you learned about God's presence in these situations?
3. If those circumstances were colors or textures in your tapestry of life, what would they look like?
4. When you look at chaotic experiences from the perspective of heaven, looking at the lifeline of your earthly life, what do they look like?
5. How might you help a friend make sense of upsets in their own lives?

The Scarlet Fiber

A cord of three strands is not quickly broken.

Ecclesiastes 4:12 (NIV)

The scarlet fiber of Jesus in my life started early in the garden of my natural parents. Though they were pretty silent about faith, they provided a way for me to find my own. They gave me a Bible, and my dad made me a beautiful cherry wood cross to hang over my bed. They also encouraged me when I wanted to join the choir at church. The thread had already been woven into my life at an early age. Everything I did affected that scarlet fiber. And that scarlet fiber in turn affected everything I did—even when I was not aware. Flash forward twenty years.

Rediscovery

It was 1979, and Rick and I had just celebrated our first anniversary. We were experiencing growing pains in our marriage, and they were intense. We realized we needed some help with our family, which included Robbie, eight, and Rusty, five, who were the cute, blond sons I inherited in our marriage. I loved these little guys and their dad so much, but I was having trouble becoming the parent the boys needed.

During that season, Rick had befriended a young man at work who had begun speaking to him about faith, God, and Jesus. Rick would bring booklets home to read, but I was not interested. Soon Rick began to change. It was not long before he gave his life to God and began to read the Bible. Meanwhile, I kept reading parenting books, making Rick go to parenting workshops with me, and desperately looking for answers.

Rick's demeanor changed. He quit drinking and partying with work buddies and started being home with the family more. He was content with life and attentive with the boys. He treated me differently, too. Not that he ever treated me badly, but suddenly I felt his love increasing.

One particularly hard, exasperating day with our too-big family in our too-little mobile home, I locked myself in the only bathroom and filled the tub with hot water. "Lord," I prayed, "I don't understand what You did on the cross and how that brings me salvation.

Intellectually, I will never understand it. It doesn't make sense to me. But, God, I want what Rick has. I'm sorry for the mistakes I've made and the things I've done that You didn't like. I remember somewhere in the Bible it says You want us to come to You as a child. So I come to You as *Your* child. I give my life to You. I can't do it alone anymore. Amen."

That was it. It truly was an act of surrender. I knew that I couldn't make things work. I couldn't make my life feel right. I needed help, and I needed it right away. Desperation consumed me.

Though I had been raised in the Presbyterian Church and had said similar words of faith in unison with the congregation, I never personally prayed to God this type of prayer.

No, I didn't see bright colors or have an epiphany experience. But there, while soaking in the tub, a peace came over me. I knew something had changed.

Our life raising our boys and later two girls had ups and downs and turns and turmoil, just as many families experience—especially blended families. But God partnered with us and together we faithfully brought our children up until they themselves gave their lives to Him on their own. God has been faithful. We are living proof that He blesses the prayers of parents over their children.

What Jesus Did for You

For many years, both before and after the bathtub prayer, hearing words like *redemption*, *repentance*, *forgiveness*, *restoration*, *reconciliation*, and *salvation* turned my stomach, filling me with shame and dread that would make my skin crawl. Why?

It's easy for us to throw around religious words, thinking everyone understands. I, for one, did not understand until I experienced their true power.

We must refuse to be numbed to the glorious things that Jesus did for us because of an offense for people who judgmentally and sometimes unconsciously made us feel ignorant.

Can I somehow help you understand these words that have so much meaning in the Bible? May I ask you to open your heart, turn off any harsh memories, and listen just for a moment? The Lord of your life is singing to you songs of honor and love. He loves you so much. These are His gifts to you!

> *Redemption* – To be redeemed is to be purchased and set free—from dark to light, from death to life, from bondage to freedom. Jesus forever paid this price so we could all be together in heaven. There was only one way to do it—a sacrifice of One who was without sin. He gladly and painfully died on the cross for the joy set before Him.
>
> That joy is life with His Father, and life with us in heaven as well as in His kingdom on earth. He is our good God.
>
> *Repentance* – All He asks of us is to repent. That only means to change the way we think about things. We change from an earthly, lonely perspective to a perspective that is from the kingdom of God. It's fresh and has as much

wisdom in it as you ask Him for. We live *from* eternity, *from* freedom, *from* heaven, and with the power and authority given to us as children of the Creator of the universe. Why wouldn't we want to change the way we think and, in the process, easily change the way we live?

Forgiveness – Every living person has sinned. The Bible tells us sin was our inheritance since the very first people on earth. Adam and Eve sinned, and there was nothing we could do to stop or change what they did.

But there was something God could do, and He did it. He loved us and made a way for us to be with Him. The Father in heaven who cannot look upon sin sent His Son, Jesus, as a perfect sacrifice. The man that had no sin suffered the penalty that we deserved. We need only to confess our sin, realizing we are not alone. When we confess, He forgives, and our slate is wiped clean. Confessing is about healing our soul and humbling our attitude. It's then that God is able to truly work in us what He desired for us from the beginning.

Restoration – What have we been restored to? When we give our lives to Christ, we are positioned supernaturally into the life God wanted for Adam and Eve—a true relationship with our heavenly Father, tending His creation and walking in fullness of friendship with Him. It's an adventure that is for us here on earth as well as after our earthly life ends.

Reconciliation – This is simply the beautiful word that assures us that Christ's sacrifice was enough for all of us to be in right relationship with our loving Father. The wall between us was forever destroyed by the Son's precious love for God and for us.

Salvation – What are we saved from and to? We are saved from death, hell, and the influence of a spiritual being that was cast out of heaven by God when he thought he could compete with God. It sounds strange, but it is real. There is a spiritual fight for our souls. We are saved to an abundant life here on earth—a life lived in the reality of God, Jesus, and Holy Spirit in us and with us. Abundance flows as we partner with God to advance His kingdom on earth. And we are saved to eternal life in heaven with Father, Son, and Holy Spirit.

What Else Did He Give Us?

Love – God is love. He, *in us*, is love. Our life is a reflection of His love. He is our Father. He embraces us, honors us, calls us friend, and as His adopted children, He gives us access to all the resources of heaven. Nothing is impossible with God.

Purity – When we give our lives to Christ, we take on His purity. Our sins were dealt with at the cross, once and for all. Once! We are His beloved. He is returning for His spotless bride, His Church.

Grace – The enabling power of God. His grace allows us to do the impossible with Him. Our lives become miraculous as we walk out His purposes and destiny for us. We begin to see His hand in everything we do, think, and experience. With God's enabling power in us, life becomes an adventure.

Joy – God is a happy God. We reflect His joy when we smile, laugh, enjoy each other, and are thankful. And God doesn't mind a good guffaw. He has a sense of humor. He laughs and dances and loves a good joke. We are made in His image. It's okay to act like Him!

Presence – Jesus practiced the presence of God and showed us how to do it. Whatever Jesus did, it's okay for us to do. Jesus spent time talking with His Papa God. He went to the mountain. He would stay up all night and pray. The miracles He delivered were empowered in those quiet moments between Father and Son. In the presence of the Father, we, too, are refreshed, restored, and recharged.

There are so many more words and definitions. Please don't ignore them like I did. No matter how they were presented to you in the past, look at them anew. In their freshness and love, recognize them as kisses from your heavenly Father. The language of the Bible, the ministry of hope, the witness of a life really lived, and the good news gospel are messages of truth and light and life and love and promise and hope and freedom. If something keeps whispering in your ear, telling you

you're incapable of understanding, ignore it. Tell it to go. Call it a liar. Then turn and trust God, and ask Him for the understanding. He will give it to you.

> But you have an anointing from the Holy One, and all of you know the truth. I do not write to you because you do not know the truth, but because you do know it and because no lie comes from the truth...the anointing you received from him remains in you, and you do not need anyone to teach you. But as his anointing teaches you about all things and as that anointing is real, not counterfeit—just as it has taught you, remain in him.
>
> 1 John 2:20-21, 27 (NIV)

Finally, those of us who have become accustomed to these wonderful words of life, let us now be refreshed in them, walk in them, and teach them as Jesus did through demonstrations of His power and grace—the same yesterday, today, and forever.

Like me, you may not have given your life to Christ until far into your adulthood, but that doesn't mean He wasn't in your life before that. He accepts you. You were His before you were born. It is the same for those who so need to hear your words today.

That scarlet fiber representing His blood protected you, healed you, and set you free, even when your conscious experience didn't match up with it. The Bible tells us that God sees the end from the beginning. You were His before you called Him yours.

A Blessing for You

I bless you now to know beyond a shadow of a doubt the truth about who you are, who you belong to, and how good your Father in heaven is. This is the truth that the Bible says will set you free. The truth is a person. It is Jesus, the Son of God. You, too, are an adopted son or daughter. He is proud of you. He will reveal everything to you. Receive the truth.

Reflect and Receive

1. When did you first know about Jesus Christ, the Son of God?
2. When did you first understand all He wanted to do for you?
3. How is the scarlet thread woven through your own life?
4. What truths have you now discovered by experience, or by reading this book?
5. What questions do you have for God? Ask them. Listen to His reply. Write it down.
6. If you were led astray, or made to feel ignorant by a church teacher or leader, take time to pray for them and forgive them, and take joy in your new season of truth, light, life, and love.

The Painter's Perspective

Write the vision
And make *it* plain on tablets,
That he may run who reads it.

Habakkuk 2:2 (NKJV)

It's about at this place in my writing where I get so wrapped up in the thoughts, stories, random ideas, and my overwhelmingly confused state of mind that I stop writing.

Why? As I step back and look at my work, rereading and editing and taking notes, I get caught up in negative thoughts:

No one will care. No one will read this. It's all about me. No one wants to know about me. I haven't given enough glory to God. It's not real enough. I should start over. What about the flow? I'm not smart enough to write a book. I'm not even a Bible scholar. I always forget what the Bible really says. People are going to laugh at me. Did I really see those miracles? Did God really talk to me about writing a book? Who do I think I am, anyway?

It's relentless.

That happened this past week. My loving husband knows my heart to finish this project. I like it when he asks me about how I'm doing and if I got any writing done today. The past couple of days, nursing a sinus cold and headache, I did not write a word. My excuses were that "My head hurts," "I'm not inspired," "I think (gasp) God wants me to start over," and "I need to write somewhere else other than at home."

I went through my list of negatives, and my wise friend and lover nodded and smiled and didn't say anything. That always gets me. I want someone to tell me what to do and what direction to go. Though I don't want Rick to put me on a guilt-trip for not working on it, I do want him to give me some supernatural wisdom. He could not. He simply flashed that funny smile.

Hmm.

It worked. The following day, I packed my computer and notebook in the Tahoe and headed to a new city to find a bookstore/coffee shop. *I'll be inspired there*, I thought.

Not only did I have to maneuver around an unfamiliar city, but I enjoyed playing with my phone's GPS and exploring what I found to be a pretty new place with loads of possibilities for future Christmas shopping.

After getting my bike wheels trued by a mechanic at a friendly bike shop adjacent to Colorado Mesa University, I headed to Barnes and Noble for a frappuccino and some creative work.

I was not disappointed. At last I had found a good place to work in this new region we moved to. I found a new book to read for a little bit of inspiration and discovered the author to be fascinating. *Amazing writing*, I thought, *but too melancholy*. The author was so talented and creative, yet there was such a despair and sadness in her voice that it almost overwhelmed and defeated my normally joyful spirit. Talk about making a reader *feel*.

It's strange. I want so much to write with flair and pizzazz and use language in amazing metaphors of color and life. Yet, when I read some of these writers, all their awesome creativity seems swallowed up in a paralyzing and sad script of life. Good writing stirs your senses, happy and sad, doesn't it?

I want to be real and gutsy, exposing my life and my soul on white pages before me, making people laugh with joy and cry with pain. But I have found so much freedom in the newness of my life with God that I really cannot go back to the sad parts very easily. It's not that I'm being pie-in-the-sky happy or mind-over-matter dishonest. No. I'm truly happy, and the rest is just not that important now.

I want so much to relate to you, and a good writer tells a story a reader can find themselves in. So I'm doing my best here. Please know that through my life's pain and struggle, losses and heartbreaks, physical pain, failures and broken dreams, I have indeed felt about all there is to feel to the point of extreme sadness and despair.

But the point of this journal I have placed in your hands is to bring light to your darkness, peace to your turmoil, truth that exposes lies you have been believing, life that injects oxygen and energy into that which is dying, and love that is more than anything you could ever imagine.

That is my message.

"But," you ask, "what if I enter into that light and then it all goes away?" My answer is simple. I want this book to give you the keys to unlock your body, soul, and spirit so you can truly partner with God in all that He wants you to enter into from this day forward.

Point of View

We sometimes feel we are in the middle of a mess: good things have come and gone, while bad things seem to find us. We make poor decisions, but sometimes we find some success. Some dreams don't make it, but some wishes come true. It all seems disorganized and confusing. Yet God, our Maker, sees it all from the perspective of the throne room. He promises to use everything for our good. He longs for us to want that. He loves us as His children. He disciplines us kindly so we will grow and fulfill our destiny. From His perspective, we are doing just fine. From His perspective, His finest creation is forming into something beautiful.

Self Portrait

Take a moment now; ask God to show you Himself in your life. Then wait and listen, and become aware of Him. He longs for these intimate moments. And there is something in you that longs for them, too. Rest. Seek. He will come. You will see His face in your spirit.

Sometimes we think we have to pray constantly or God won't show up. God calls us His friend. Friends converse. If we are praying constantly, God can't speak. Be silent. Let Him communicate with you. Remember, He will speak to you through His still, small voice, sometimes an audible voice, thoughts, the Bible, friends, music, dreams, creativity, and signs.

Watch and be aware as you go through your days. Keep a journal of prayers and answers, praises and thankfulness. Can you see the designs God is weaving around your life?

He is still creating.

A Blessing for You

I bless you to have the courage to climb the mountain to see your life's experience, and even yourself, from the perspective of heaven. I bless you to find new purpose, supernatural strength to continue on your course, and a new sense of wisdom to maneuver through your life.

Reflect and Receive

1. Is there anything you would tell God if He was standing in front of you? Tell Him now. Don't be afraid that He won't like what you say. Ask Him the hard stuff, too. He can handle it. He wants to handle it. Ask Him to help you know Him more.
2. What do you think you look like to God?
3. What does your life look like to God?
4. Can you see a pattern of experiences, risks, skills, gifts, and talents that seems to be moving you toward something? If so, what do you think that something might be?

The Finishing Touches

Guide me in your truth and teach me, for you are God my Savior, and my hope is in you all day long.

Psalm 25:5 (NIV)

It was a cold December night in 2008.

My daughter Erin and grandson Trey were with me on Berthoud Pass, driving back from Denver.

The aftermath of my outpatient breast biopsy was throbbing and painful, with bandages wrapped tight to control bleeding.

As I drove my Ford Freestyle around the switchbacks and curves, the icy roads necessitated slowing. I had driven this pass countless times since 1974 when I first moved to Winter Park, which sits at the west end of the pass. We were driving and talking, and my two-year-old grandson was in his car seat in the back, playing.

It happened quickly; a car driving toward me on the narrow road slid into my path and spun. There was no time to avoid him. I smashed square into the side of his car. My grandson screamed, the airbags exploded, and smoke filled my car. Panicked, we got out of the car quickly into the below-zero night to wait for the state patrol.

Thankfully, there were no serious injuries. The boys that had been driving in the other car were from South America and touring Colorado before they began work in Vail. Their rental car was badly damaged. My car was totaled.

This would not be that remarkable of a story if it weren't for some other events in my life. I have mentioned the other car accident I had several years before. Though this recent one was not my fault, it tended to give me a great deal of anxiety. The what-ifs were coming at me. I felt vulnerable and exposed and felt strangely like someone was out to kill me.

The other thing that made this remarkable was the timing. It happened at the same time that we broke down financially. Within a three-month period, we had filed for bankruptcy, lost our business, been laid off two jobs, faced foreclosure on our home, and felt quite financially hopeless. And now there was the looming breast biopsy report. This accident threatened to drive me over the edge of sanity.

I was thankful that Erin and Trey were not hurt, just shaken. Trey kept talking about the loud boom. Soon he and my daughter were whisked back to our warm house by a kindly passer-by while I waited for the police. The driver of the car that hit us came to see how we were. I assured him we were okay, although I knew I was shaken and whiplashed.

I have to admit, I did wonder what it was all about and why all these things were happening. It would have been easy for me to feel very sorry for myself. After all, everyone else was feeling very sorry for us. But what was in my heart to do most of all was thank God for His protection and to pray for the boys in the other car.

By this stage in my life, after going around and around the turmoil and joys of living, I had learned to see my life from a better perspective. I had finally begun to have a habit of looking for what God was doing.

I know this sounds strange, but He *was* doing something. He did not cause that accident. He is good, and there is no evil in Him. Accidents happen. There are earthly laws of gravity and ice, speed and inexperience.

As this event unfolded over the coming months, it turned out that a small settlement from the rental car agency helped fund some of our ministry school expenses. Coincidence? I really don't think so. The timing was perfect. The check came as we left for school in September. My whiplash? Thanks to chiropractic and healing prayer, I am totally healed.

And the biopsy? Negative.

Molding and Shaping

I love the Internet. I love all the information I have at my fingertips. I love the interaction with friends on e-mail, Facebook, and Skype. I love my MacBook Pro!

There are some things I *don't* love about the Internet. As a journalist, I am sad at the cultural shift away from newspapers that the Internet has caused. I am sad that so many newspapers are out of business and journalists—good journalists—are jobless. I am sad that children find more fun playing by themselves on the computer than interacting with family over a board game. I am sad that people no longer write personal, hand-scripted letters, mailed with a pretty stamp at the post office.

I am sad that people no longer get quality news because they read it in good newspapers. Now they expect to get just the news they want to read on the Internet.

I am sad that the Internet is used by creeps. Some people spend their lives spewing lies and political garbage, preying on websites and online newspaper stories.

Probably what makes me most sad are the map services on the Internet that cause me to get lost.

You might see I'm segueing into something here. Many of us have gone down the wrong roads in life again and again. We feel lost and misdirected. We may feel like we missed out on our calling or gifting, choosing to work a job we didn't like because of the money. Or we listened to the wrong teaching on politics or church and followed that road for too long, only to be hurt or deceived. Or we may have been right where we wanted to be—raising our family, enjoying our life—but now things are different. The kids are grown and gone, our job skills are rusty at best, and we have no idea what to do next. We're too old to start again and too young to give up and die.

If you've been feeling like you missed the boat, stop it! Don't let another day steal your dreams and joy. You have not missed any boats no matter how old you are or what your circumstance. Yes, you may have made choices you would change now, but those were the choices you made based on the best information you had.

Can I ask you a question?

Did you do the best you knew how?

If your answer is yes, then stop regretting the past, and start looking at the future. God's map is perfect. You have many years left to offer all of yourself to whatever you desire in your heart to do. God puts those desires in you. He wants to partner with you to make them happen.

Do whatever it takes. Take a class, start an interest group, learn the computer, and begin to pray to the God who created you and ask Him what you two are going to do next.

Then watch for Him to begin to work in your life through an amazing array of creativity in thought and planning. You may have divine appointments with people who could help you learn skills, fund an invention, or make a dream come true.

God is the God of the impossible. If you are looking at your life and your dreams in the "impossible realm," He is ready for you.

> Now to him who is able to do immeasurably more than all we ask or imagine, according to his power that is at work within us, to him be glory in the church and in Christ Jesus throughout all generations, for ever and ever!
>
> Ephesians 3:20-21 (NIV)

Strokes of the Supernatural

I have a friend named Daniel. He's from Germany, and I met him at ministry school. He is an amazing revivalist and evangelist and is touching many homeless and drug culture people in his neighborhood. He has prayed for them and experienced miracles of healing, deliverance, and salvation.

One evening, Daniel was lying on his bed, talking to God about his need for a MacBook Pro computer and Adobe software so he could produce his digital paintings. He also prayed that God would send people to his door that needed ministry.

The next morning, Daniel was awakened by a phone call. Since it was an 800 number, he almost didn't answer; but after a few rings, he said hello.

"This is the Apple Computer Company. Is this Daniel?" a kind voice asked.

Daniel shook his head in surprise and sat up in bed. "Yes," he said steadily.

"We have a customer that asked us to call you. This person would like you to order anything you want from us, and it will be paid for."

Daniel couldn't believe what he was hearing. Was this real or a hoax?

He began to order. "Yes, I would like a MacBook Pro and Adobe products including…" Daniel continued to order what he would need for his digital art. The operator took the order and Daniel's address, said good-bye, and hung up.

Later that day, there was a knock on the door. A man stood there asking if Daniel could talk and answer some questions about his life. Daniel knew God had sent this man in answer to his prayer for souls to come to his door.

In Daniel's words:

"He broke out in tears at my door and then gave his life to Jesus in my living room and got baptized in the Holy Spirit after a three-hour conversation. His wife even came to my house a few days later to ask what happened to her husband, because he was so transformed and full of joy."[2]

Daniel knew then that God was bringing him into a season of "effortless fruitfulness" in his ministry.

Within three weeks, to his great delight, the MacBook Pro was delivered to his door, and the package included the most elite and powerful model of the laptop computer and the new Adobe CS5 software bundle. Daniel notes on his blog: "God certainly knows what's good!"[2]

God Is Good

We can expect and anticipate God's goodness when we pray and ask Him for help, guidance, direction, and resources.

Using these tools, Daniel continues to position himself to be used by God. He even told me that whenever he prays for someone needing a job, they get a job within a couple of days. He is ministering around the world to young people in person and by blog, teaching them to be bold, to declare their freedom in God, and showing them God is real as he teaches them to walk in demonstrations of power just like the disciples walked. Those he ministers to are witnessing healing and deliverance, and many are giving their lives to Christ.

There are so many testimonies of the power of God directed to and through His children. What are your testimonies? If you have lived very long at all, you have stories of things that have happened that can't be explained, like unusual blessings, gifts, financial miracles, good news from a doctor, a pet who brings you extreme joy, or the way you feel one morning when all looks hopeful and good. Consider that these blessings are from the Father in heaven who loves you and delights to give you gifts.

I urge you to thank God for what He is doing and will do. And I also urge you to refuse to dwell or spend time worrying about what He hasn't done yet.

Culinary Art

You know that wonderful lemonade they sell at county fairs? It's the kind with real lemons and cane sugar and just the right amount of mixing and shaking, poured out with ice, and served with slices of lemon and sugar around the lip of the cup, ready to refresh a very thirsty soul.

Yes, that's my favorite fair drink. One of our local restaurants is starting to sell it. It's not quite the same, because the lemons aren't inside the glass. When I ordered the natural lemonade on the menu, the young man asked if I wanted light or natural. I asked what the light was, and he said it was artificially sweetened for those who want no calories. "No, no, no!" I answered. "I want the *real* lemonade!"

I feel most of my adult life has been too much about avoiding the natural and going after the artificial— food, soda pop, fabrics, flavors, decreased fat, processed, diet, fake, blah!

What about authentic? In my quest to be the real me, I am beginning to desire the real stuff. Natural lemonade made with real lemons and sugar. Natural, organic meat and vegetables grown without chemicals and hormones. And real cotton and silk, even if I have to iron. This goes for cosmetics, vitamins, protein powders, and cereals. Although we are on a strict budget, I am willing to pay at least a little extra for the real stuff.

And this same trend goes for my beliefs, too. Many churches I have experienced have distorted the pure message of the Bible. The Word has been watered down and sugared up to the point it doesn't look, feel, smell, or taste real. In an effort to please everyone, some teachers have avoided certain topics or taken a different route around an issue or ignored hazards, hoping they would go away.

So what is real? What are we supposed to believe?

Is the Bible true and right? What about when it contradicts itself? What about history and the church? What about the Bible scholars? Can I trust myself to know what is right, or do I need someone to tell me?

The church quite often keeps busy answering questions that people are not asking.

I don't have all the answers for you other than my own understanding after praying and asking God to show me. I feel these are questions you need to sincerely come before God about.

But here are some of my personal responses to the above questions.

Is the Tome True?

The writers of the Bible were witnesses, humans like you and me, inspired, selected, and used by God to deliver His story and His message to His children.

The Bible is true. Yes, it contradicts itself sometimes, but in those times we can seek our Father for revelation and trust Him to show us living truth. The reason you can read the Bible again and again and get totally different understanding, wisdom and "aha" moments is because it is indeed a Living Word. God has hidden things in there for us to find in the right season. What a wonderful way He has of communicating with us.

What about Church History?

The history of the church is a history that has depended too much on the wisdom of man and too little on the wisdom of God. James 5:1 says we can ask for wisdom and He will give it generously. Ask. Listen. Then believe. If we can go to the root of the beginnings of the church, we will discover the purity and simplicity of what Jesus Himself taught. I urge you again to read the Gospel of John and the book of Acts. Read Hebrews, too. It's all in there.

The Teaching of Bible Scholars

I thank the Lord for Bible scholars. Through the years, I have read many books by authors who know more than me, and I have loved most of these books. They helped me gain new perspectives on my Bible reading.

My first Bible was a King James Version, and I started it many times as a teen and never got past Genesis. I didn't know then that I could start at other places in this big book. It wasn't until the Holy Spirit came to me in power that the Bible became a Living Word in my life, nourishing and feeding me with each day's reading.

The Holy Spirit stands by, waiting for us to ask Him for help. Jesus sent this helper to remind us of all that He taught and to be our counselor. Just ask.

Can I Trust Myself to Know What Is True?

How do you trust yourself to know what is right and what to believe? With God all things are possible. Put your trust in Him to show you. Ask for His wisdom. Sense His nudges.

Finally, again, you can trust yourself because the Holy Spirit is in you, and you can believe you have received the wisdom you have asked God for.

God sends us people to help us. Sometimes they are divine appointments, like Philip stopping for the Ethiopian Eunuch in Acts chapter 8. Other times the ones He sends are those we love who are around us all the time. They may be leaders in our church or our pastor. Listen to their counsel. Pray that you will learn to discern what is right and good and let go of what doesn't seem right.

You are made in the image of God. You have been given the mind of Christ. These are promises in the Bible. Now, move forward and function in what God is giving you to do.

What Will You Do?

This past year, I have been reading biographies of people who led moves of God in the past 100 years. These were men and women called and empowered by God to deliver His love and minister His healing.

The book I'm reading now is about William Branham, who ministered in the years after World War II. He claimed he was just a normal brother in Christ and credited every healing to Jesus, reminding the people that Jesus was "the same yesterday, today, and forever," and therefore now present to heal them.

Many thousands who came to his meetings around the world were physically healed. One former US congressman walked after being paralyzed for sixty-five years. Others near death with cancer went on to live long lives. Sometimes cancerous tumors fell off of the body and were visible to everyone. A boy dead for half an hour after being hit by a car was raised to life, and his critical injuries were healed as people watched. Some healings were immediate. Others happened over time and were later confirmed.

John G. Lake is another leader who ministered in the early 1900s. A successful businessman and investor, he gave up everything to follow God's call to impart healing and bring salvation to Africa and the United States. He would go on to start healing rooms on the US West Coast where divine healings were so numerous that hospitals were literally emptied.

Jesus showed us how to live and walk, and He taught us how to pray. He is still present to heal and deliver, and He wants to do it through us.

God continues to call and empower men and women to service. Many prophets are declaring there is a new move of God, a revival, already under way. The harvest will need many workers.

This is a significant hour. We need to believe, to pray, to prepare, and to watch what God is doing.

There are so many ways to be involved today, from giving and tithing, to serving in missions, to using your God-given gifts and talents for your community.

If you are wondering if God is calling you to this important work, the answer is yes.

A Blessing for You

Psalm 145:18 promises the Lord is near to all who call on Him in truth. I bless you to have a sincere and open heart and spirit to receive in humility and truth all that God wants to tell you. I bless you to know and have it confirmed the promises He speaks to you through His living word, written and revealed to you. I bless you to know the protection of your Father in heaven, who will guide you on the right path toward understanding and knowing His nature.

Reflect and Receive

1. God has given you a unique imagination to be used to know Him more. How is your imagination teaching you?
2. How has your upbringing influenced your own walk of faith?
3. Have you discovered any beliefs about God changing as you experience life and relate to others?

4. Affirm now what He has given you. Declare over yourself who you are, what your gifts are, and call it "good," as God has already done. He is still creating you and creating with you.

The Masterpiece

You Are God's Artwork

> Yet you, Lord, are our Father. We are the clay, you are the potter; we are all the work of your hand.
>
> Isaiah 64:8 (NIV)

God's paintbrush dabs rainbow colors on the canvas of creation.

The divine Potter brushes a golden glaze onto His earthen vessel that will provide just the right sheen.

The master Weaver stands back to gaze at the almost finished masterpiece and imagines just where He might place it for the best visibility.

You are God's creation. You are His vessel. You are the masterpiece. He did have a plan before He began

His work on you, and He still has a plan for the finished piece.

You are freshly made and nearly complete. He is saying over you, "It is good!"

Your life is like the earth's ages. He completed the earth in seven days, but it was not the end of the story. The earth was ready to receive man and to host all that God had planned for it.

God sees the end from the beginning as He watches the lives of His children unfold. He waits for His love for them to be discovered and hopes it will be returned. He made the earth for us. For man and woman, His friends. He desires our love on our terms, for He created love, and it is only precious in its power to be felt and given. Love can't be made up, imagined, or retained without a spark of supernatural power.

If we are made in His image, shouldn't we believe that love means everything to Him as it does to us? Is His a love that can forgive, touch, heal, suffer, and survive great loss? Is it a love that can overcome a broken heart, be filled with compassion for the hurting, and be jealous for purity?

Yes! Most of us have experienced this love in human form. We can be sure God has experienced this love among His Trinity relationship of Father, Son, and Holy Spirit. Most importantly, though, we need to understand with hearts of openness and belief that God experiences that type of love *with* us. He feels that way toward us, and He extends that type of love to others through us.

We are spiritual beings living an earthly existence. That means our spirit is in communion with God because He is spirit. And we are always meant to be in communion with His love, because God is love.

On a human, physical level, we can be aware of this. In our resting moments with our Father in heaven, we can ask Him to show us this type of pure love. As He fills us up, we in turn are compelled to love others because, in doing so, we love Him back.

Finishing the Work

My own life's tapestry made by my heavenly Father is almost finished. It doesn't mean it's the end of my life on earth. It means I'm ready. He's done His work in me. My experience has developed a firm foundation and springboard. The masterpiece of my life is about ready to go on tour.

What could it mean? I think it may have to do with my dreams—dreams of travel, fun, family, friends, and a big ministry goal of bringing a message of love and hope to the spiritually hungry. I am so excited about this launch. Like a caterpillar in a cocoon—or an almost done tapestry—I am in a season of waiting. I know something is imminent. I am so excited to find out what it is. Yet, I am content and at peace in the waiting.

Pedicures and Epiphanies

I love to say the word *epiphany*.

I fancy the way it sounds. It is big and musical, like the word *symphony*. It tickles my tongue and lips and brightens my senses like a chocolate ice cream cone on a hot, muggy day.

It has a few meanings, but for my purposes here, I'll take this definition from my online dictionary: "A sudden, intuitive perception of or insight into the reality or essential meaning of something, usually initiated by some simple, homely, or commonplace occurrence or experience."

I had an epiphany just the other day at the grocery store.

I was walking down an aisle past diapers, thinking, *Oh, I am so glad those days are over.* Then I passed the feminine products, and, once again, I thought, *Oh, I am so glad those days are over.*

Feeling pretty happy and a little smug about it all, I proceeded to the hair dye, then the moisturizing eye drops, the ibuprofen, and the anti-wrinkle cream. I also spent a little time thinking about the pedicure that was way overdue and my thick toenails that were becoming increasingly contrary.

Suddenly, I gasped, screaming silently. Was I getting *old?*

That was an odd epiphany and except for the smug moment, not very happy.

Here is another one:

Hurricane Irene was pounding the East Coast, and the news media was issuing warnings to take cover, to evacuate, that the worst was yet to come.

At the time, I had been reading about five Psalms a day. It just so "happened" that on this day of seeming doom, I read Psalm 107:9: "He stilled the storm to a whisper, the waves of the sea were hushed."

I prayed that over the storm. I have learned that in times of disaster, it is good to intercede with prayers for protection for people. It is also good to speak to the storm as Jesus did. "Peace, be still." Jesus gives us authority over the earth to do as He did and more. (See Mark 4:39, NKJV.)

Soon after I prayed, I received a Facebook plea from my friend Molly, asking for prayers for her family members and friends in the path of the storm. I sent her back the verse, and she in turn sent it on to more people.

I believe God not only had me read and share that verse so we could intercede in the storm, but He was also showing me this was His promise over the storm. That was my epiphany. He was foretelling what He was going to do, and I could trust it and share it.

The storm did a lot of damage, but I believe God did calm the storm and the waves as people prayed. There was less damage and loss of life than the dire predictions warned. The hurricane calmed to a tropical storm. While ocean surges went on to cause much flooding, we will never fully know what might have been had we and many others *not* interceded and called on the power and protection of the Almighty.

I grieve for the ones who lost loved ones and property, but I am thankful for the mighty protection of life over this region.

Tragedies and natural disasters respond to the prayers of the faithful, but our intercession can also make a difference in the practical realms of life. We can pray and declare "peace, be still" over our homes, families, jobs, health, and finances.

Peace and Money

In the past few years, I have learned and studied about money from God's perspective. How are we to manage it, use it, and grow it? How are we to think about it?

My heart aches for my kids sometimes as I see them facing some of the same tough challenges their dad and I faced over the years. I want to say so much to them, to teach them, and to help them understand our way was not always the right way. One part of me says, *Don't interfere*, while another one screams, *Interfere! Interfere!*

I know there are a lot of lessons we all need to learn for ourselves, but why can't our ceiling be our childrens' floor? Why do we need to see them fight the same battles and cover the same ground we already paid such a dear price to conquer?

Another part of me is saying, *They don't have to. Write it down for them and for their children and for their children's children.* Paul and some of the disciples did it. I can, too.

Prosperity

I want to share this letter with my children and my readers, in prayer that it may somehow encourage you and that you, too, may know my heart more intimately.

Dear Loved Ones,

This letter concerns money and your soul.

The Bible says, "May you prosper as your soul prospers," (3 John, 1-2).

What does that mean?

First, Papa Rick and I need you to know we love you more than you could ever imagine. We have been through much together. Sometimes you knew our struggles as a couple as we raised you. Sometimes we protected you from knowing those struggles.

We are so proud of how you are living your lives, raising your children, and reaching for your dreams.

You amaze us as we see you teaching your own kids things we wish we had learned earlier and taught you.

God is so good to us through you.

We want you to understand how there is an enemy out there who lies about money and life. These lies include such things as:

- There is never enough.
- I am all alone in this world.
- Money is the answer to everything.
- Our children deserve it all.
- If I don't do this myself, no one will ever help me do it.
- You have to spend money to make money (this is not always a lie but can be deceiving).
- Debt is good and builds your credit.

- We have to work ourselves to death to make it.
- My dreams are not important.
- I have to stay in a job I don't like to make it in this world.
- Being a responsible Christian means I can't have any fun and have to be miserable and have a sour face. (Okay, I added that for fun.)

Before I go on, I need you to understand that money is not evil. It is a wonderful tool God provides to us for His purposes in our lives. We have a problem when there is a love of money or when we allow it to control us.

You may have more lies to add to the list. Regretfully, Rick and I got caught up in these lies and taught you about some of them through our actions and words. I believe we learned some of these things from our parents and they from theirs.

Lies are based in fear. There is a poverty spirit that says, "There is never enough." There is an orphan spirit that says, "It's just me against the world." There is a spirit of mammon that says, "Money is power and will answer all of my problems." It tries to replace God with money.

I want to break these destructive beliefs now in your life with God's help.

First, you need to remember who you are and whose you are. If you have truly given your life to Jesus, then you are a child of the living God, the Creator of the universe, who created you in His image and gave you a purpose and a destiny. You are coheirs with Christ. You rule with Him as kings and queens, royalty in a kingdom that Jesus asked us to advance here on earth, just like the prayer says, "On earth as it is in heaven."

As coheirs with Christ, you have access to all the riches and resources of heaven. The Bible says God owns the cattle on a thousand hills (see Psalm 50:10). All belongs to Him. All means all. Your paycheck belongs to Him, too. He generously gives you the means to live the life He has placed you in. When you realize who you are and that you belong to Him, you realize you can ask Him for what you need and expect Him to provide.

He asks only that we give back a tithe—10 percent. We get to keep ninety percent. It's not for Him. He doesn't need money. It's more about our attitude, learning, and understanding that as we give others can be blessed. As we give, we take our hands of control off and learn to trust God with more than our money.

It's about being generous as He has been generous with us. He says in His Word we can test Him in this:

> Bring your full tithe to the Temple treasury so there will be ample provisions in my Temple. Test me in this, and see if I don't open up heaven itself to you and pour out blessings beyond your wildest dreams.
>
> Malachi 3:10, (The Message)

We can't out-give God. Do test Him in this. You can expect blessing upon blessing. Just ask us. We will tell you of God's supernatural provision in ways that seemed impossible as we ourselves tested him in this area of giving. This goes for more than money. As you bless others with love, compassion, help, and prayer, God will begin to pour abundance into your life.

He calls us friends. He has revealed His secrets to us in His Word and demonstrated the way we are to carry out His purposes. It *is* an adventure.

God purchased us for a big price—the life of His beloved Son, Jesus. Don't you want to find out why?

Do you know how much He loves you? Your heavenly Father wants to shower you with His gifts and blessings. He is waiting for you to understand the wisdom of having a generous spirit.

We are adopted into His family. We are not alone, and we are not orphans. It never has been "just me against the world." No. We are members of a family in God, and we are called into the family business.

Second, the spirit of poverty says "there is never enough." It makes us strive and work and sweat and spend enough to prove itself so we strive and work and sweat some more.

The prosperous soul understands "there is more than enough." This is a kingdom truth that is understood when we know who we are, whose we are, and what we have access to as royal heirs of the kingdom. As we receive this truth, we become thankful to God for what He gives us, not worrying about what we don't have yet. We learn to give generously and budget what we have. We trust God to provide for us. We wait sometimes for what we want, and sometimes that want or need loses its power over us. We learn to save. We avoid the curse of debt and credit and learn to manage it instead of allowing it to manage us. Rick and I are still learning this lesson, so my words here are to declare these truths over the two of us as well.

It is always a good day to start this thinking and plan to change. God will bless it in ways you will never imagine. He will bless it by not only meeting your needs but by giving you surprises—financial as well as in relationships and miracles.

This is the way of repentance. Repentance simply means changing the way we think. When we do, our former ways that held us in bondage will be rendered powerless.

Focus on God, not money.

Focus on freedom, not bondage.

Focus on prosperity and promise, not lack.

Focus on the royalty you are, not on the prisoner the enemy would have you believe you are.

There are resource books listed in the back of this book to help you on this road.

Some of you are in the years when your children's activities keep you running. Still others are ready to step into your destiny. This message is for all of you. We remember the striving, the fear, the feeling we couldn't ever save anything for the future, wondering what would become of us and of you.

The worst happened to us financially, but it was not the worst. Our poverty mentality would have us live as failures, depressed, and beaten down. We have killed that spirit and welcomed a new way of thinking that says, "We have a new start, another chance to do it right. We have each other. We are victors over that rat race that held us in its grips for too long. We *will* make it, and we *will* be able to leave an inheritance for our children."

This is part of your inheritance. We not only want to leave your inheritance in a bank account to help you reach yours and God's dreams for you and your children and your grandchildren, but we want to leave a legacy of victory for you that will forever impact our family as you yourselves pass it to future generations. Hear my prayer for you, my own children and my spiritual children, and you who are reading this book. Those of you who are parents and grandparents, I share this with you as you pray it over your own:

> So Lord, our provider and protector, we pray for our precious ones down through the generations, and we ask for You to give them strength and wisdom as they consider Your will for their prosperity. We pray that they would prosper as their souls prosper, that they would learn soon for themselves their identity in You and how very much You love them. We pray You would give them victories and that the road, though sometimes rocky, will be full of fun, joy, promise, love, and adventure as they move forward toward all that You have for them. We pray that our ceiling will be their floor and that they will see and accomplish much more than we could ever have imagined for them.
>
> We thank You, Lord, for the privilege of being their parents and grandparents, for the privilege of being allowed to pay a price so that our children could do life better than we did.

They may make new mistakes, but, please, Lord, may they not have to repeat all of our mistakes.
We love You and trust You with our family.

In Jesus's Name,
Amen

Mother's Milk

One day at Walmart, I was walking by the camping aisle when I heard a scream.

Even though I'm way past childbearing age, a baby's cry still moves me. I want to run and hold them and comfort them with kisses and reassuring words.

One time, when I was a nursing mother, I was at my bank. My baby was home with her dad. While standing in line, I began to think about my baby, and all of a sudden I started to gush milk. It was summer, and I was wearing a light top, a nursing bra, and no nursing pads. Well, it was very plain to see that the liquid forming on my shirt was not sweat. Pretending that nothing was happening, I finished my business and then headed out with two round wet spots you-know-where.

This happened frequently during my nursing seasons—in the night when I'd dream about the baby, in the day when I would hear her cry, even at stores when other babies were crying.

It is a natural, physiological response that bonds mother and baby. Even those who choose not to nurse experience it. It's in our nature. Baby cries, mother runs, and they are both satisfied as they peacefully cuddle.

If God created us this way, and we are made in His image, I think it is safe to say that He has a similar response to our cries. He "runs" to provide us with the nourishment of His Word. His desire and will are to help, to heal, and to silence our cries with His goodness.

It is a law of the kingdom:

Prayer brings response.

Hunger brings nourishment.

Distress brings relief.

God cannot listen to us without responding. He is our provider. We are His children. Like a mother leaks milk, and a daddy comforts the child He loves, God leaks Himself into the circumstances of His children.

When you are alone or scared, crying or hurt, sick or worried, let Him know. You are His baby, made in His image. It would be unnatural and inconsistent with His character to not provide you the extra love and attention you need in the moment.

He is such a good Father.

God's Embrace

I want you to imagine yourself as a tiny infant in the hands of your loving Father in heaven. He has so much planned for you. He is so pleased with how you turned out. He knows what is ahead. His heart is so full of love for you. He has put His dreams in you.

I was talking to my daughter the other day and had this overwhelming need to be a mom and "cuddle" with her on the phone.

She had just been talking about cuddling with her own sweet twenty-month-old daughter as they watched *SpongeBob SquarePants*. I remember a time twenty-eight years ago when I did the same with my twenty-month-old—only we watched videos of *Sesame Street*. Those times of heart-to-heart touching and closeness with my children are forever engraved on my heart.

As you embrace your own and your future children, know that the touch of that embrace lingers into eternity.

A Word from a Grandma

Reader, will you let me be your grandma for a moment?

This is for everyone, no matter what your age, no matter how you came upon this book, no matter if you are related to me or not. Please let me be your spiritual grandma in this moment.

These are things I wish I had learned as a child, teen, and young adult so that I could have put them into practice early in life:

You Have Been Prayed For

No matter who you are or how your life has looked until now, whether you have followed after God or you aren't quite there yet, I want you to know that somewhere in your past generations, there was someone who prayed for you and had hope for you—a grandparent, aunt, distant cousin, someone who looked at his or her family and prayed that future generations would come into the knowledge of the Creator—the God who loves them—and that you would be mightily blessed.

Who Are You?

It is no accident that you are reading this now. You are called into action—called into the heart of love that is God—and from this moment you will step into a new season of walking as the amazing creation you are. There is only one person that has ever been like you, and it's you. You don't need to look or be like anyone else. You have a divine set of traits, talents, gifts, dreams, ideas, and DNA that is exclusive. You please God most when you understand who you are, and you honor Him when you reveal that person to the world around you.

Hope

Never let go of hope. Your dreams and plans reflect God's dreams and plans for you. Your imagination is created by God, and He uses it. Begin to pray about your dreams, and develop your gifts to bring you closer to those dreams. Watch and wait, and see what God does to bring the possible to what you thought could not happen.

Joy

It's okay to be happy. There is no guilt in it, no shame in it—none. The Bible says that the kingdom of God is made up of righteousness, peace, and joy in the Holy Spirit. Joy is one third of the kingdom. Any feeling you have that does not fit into those three categories is not in the kingdom. That means fear, stress, anxiety, driven-ness, depression, striving, and anger should have no power over you as a child of God. Line yourself up with the kingdom. Be joyful, and spread joy. God is a happy God. He is good, and He is in a good mood. That should make us happy!

Creativity

God created the universe. He created this beautiful planet we live on. He created you and me. We are made in His image. That means we are created to be creative. He has sprinkled some amazing elements inside you for that very purpose. These equip you for your calling in life, and they not only bless you; they are designed to bless others.

Take a few moments and think. What do you love to do? Is it always the same as your friends? God has made you unique. You may love to paint, to speak, or to write. Or you may love to work with wood, plant trees, or try new recipes. You may love to decorate, to create atmospheres, or think beyond what most people put effort into. Do you have creative ideas for inventions? Have you discovered a new way of doing business? Do you love to help others with your creativity?

Find what it is that God has put into you. No one is exempt from this. Rick used to say he wasn't creative, yet he is one of the most creative people I know. He may not be an artist or dancer, but he does have a way with wood and words that is like no other person I know. When he is working in a shop, designing a house, or even at school writing a report, God partners with him and beautiful things emerge. That is creativity.

We all need to learn what it means to dream with God and create with God.

Bill Johnson, in *Dreaming With God* (my favorite book), says it this way:

> Creativity is a manifestation of wisdom in the context of excellence and integrity.
>
> We were born to partner with wisdom—to live in it and display it through creative expression.
>
> To embrace the privilege of creative expression is consistent with being made in the image and likeness of our Creator.

Will you discover and unwrap the special creative gifts within you? I pray that you will. And in so doing, you will learn what it means to create with God.

Fear Not

Fear is from the enemy. Fear, doubt, depression, anxiety, striving, or beating yourself up are not from God. Recognize God's truth in you. Know there is a battle for your soul. Reject negative lies that come against you through your thoughts and through other people.

Know Your Identity in God

You are a child of the King. You walk in all power and authority as representatives of the kingdom. God has put the enemy under the feet of Christ and under your feet, too. When a lie comes against you, recognize it as a lie and kill it like you would a mosquito. The devil has no power over you unless you believe his lies. How do you kill the lie? Speak the truth over yourself! There are declarations of God's promises printed at the end of this book. Declare them aloud frequently and restore the truths that overcome lies.

Trust God

Know that when you go through tough times, your loving Father is always with you. Always. He knows what you are going through. He will listen to and answer your prayers. Listen for His answers. Listen for His voice. In our moments of difficulty come times of deepening our relationship with God. This is the good that can come of these times. This is some of what Romans 8:28 talks about: "And we know that in all things God works for the good of those who love him, who have been called according to his purpose."

Learn to Forgive

In your life, people will let you down. You will get hurt. People will say things you can't forget. Circumstances may make you angry with even God. And all of us make mistakes in life that make it hard to forgive ourselves.

Forgiveness is not for the other person. It is for our own souls. When we forgive others, it takes our heart and spirit from a place of bondage and sets it free to move forward into life.

When we forgive God, we are restored to right relationship, just as when He forgave us. We are open and free to receive from Him.

When we forgive ourselves, we enter into the forgiveness of God that was already given when we received salvation. God forgives us totally across eternity. He does not want us to dwell on the past and live in depression. The enemy would have us stay there so we become totally ineffective in the advancing of the kingdom of God on earth. It's an enemy strategy. Resist it. Forgiving yourself releases you from a prison of self-pride and self-consciousness and restores your "God consciousness" so you can pursue your God-given destiny.

Love God

God created you because He wanted to know you, communicate with you, and relate to you. This book is all about how to make that connection. This is serious business. God has nothing but great and wonderful love for you. Pursue Him with your whole heart. See how He brings love into your life in so many ways, ways you could never imagine. He is always for you and never against you.

———◆———

I want to close this chapter with a psalm and a prayer. The Bible is full of such beauty in words and imagery. I could not share my heart for you in a more beauti-

ful way than with these excerpts from God's love book
to you:

> I lift up my eyes to the hills—
> Where does my help come from?
> My help comes from the Lord,
> The Maker of heaven and earth.
> He will not let your foot slip—
> He who watches over you will not slumber;
> Indeed, he who watches over Israel
> Will neither slumber nor sleep.
> The Lord watches over you –
> The Lord is your shade at your right hand;
> The sun will not harm you by day,
> Nor the moon by night.
> The Lord will keep you from all harm –
> He will watch over your life;
> The Lord will watch over your coming and going
> Both now and forevermore.
>
> Psalm 121 (NIV)

Paul's prayer to the Ephesians is also my prayer
for you:

> For this reason I kneel before the Father, from
> whom every family in heaven and on earth
> derives its name. I pray that out of his glori-
> ous riches he may strengthen you with power
> through his Spirit in your inner being, so that
> Christ may dwell in your hearts through faith.
> And I pray that you, being rooted and estab-
> lished in love, may have power, together with all

the Lord's holy people, to grasp how wide and long and high and deep is the love of Christ, and to know this love that surpasses knowledge—that you may be filled to the measure of all the fullness of God. Now to him who is able to do immeasurably more than all we ask or imagine, according to his power that is at work within us, to him be glory in the church and in Christ Jesus throughout all generations, for ever and ever! Amen.

Ephesians 3:14-20 (NIV)

A Blessing for You

I bless you to have understanding of God's life lessons for you regarding everything from purpose to prosperity; that you will know who you are in God, your identity as a child of the living Creator of the universe. You are an adopted child of a good Father, brother and sister of His son, Jesus; heir of the abundance of heaven; with a destiny to advance the kingdom of God on earth through His Holy Spirit. He calls you "friend."

Reflect and Receive

1. In the section of life lessons from a grandma, score where you are for each subject. On a scale of 1 – 5, with five being the greatest, where are you in your awareness and understanding of these important lessons?

1. You have been prayed for.
2. Who are you?
3. Hope.
4. Joy.
5. Creativity.
6. Fear not.
7. Know your identity in God.
8. Trust God.
9. Learn to forgive.
10. Love God.

2. Pray about these. Take steps to work on those that you need more wisdom and understanding about for your own life.

The Gallery

The Spirit of God, the Master, is on me because God anointed me. He sent me to preach good news to the poor, heal the heartbroken, Announce freedom to all captives, pardon all prisoners. GOD sent me to announce the year of his grace— a celebration of God's destruction of our enemies— and to comfort all who mourn, To care for the needs of all who mourn in Zion, give them bouquets of roses instead of ashes, Messages of joy instead of news of doom, a praising heart instead of a languid spirit. Rename them "Oaks of Righteousness" planted by God to display his glory.

Isaiah 61:1-7 (The Message)

Your life's tapestry is done. It's full of color, contrast, gold and red threads, high and low texture, and it shows an amazing picture of your life created by an artist's hand.

Now what?

Your tapestry may be done, but your life is not done yet.

With loving care, the tapestry will hang for a long time while you continue to live out your years. What happens next now that you have discovered what your life has been about and what God has put into you?

Your life's tapestry could "hang" in a home, and everything about it could bring love to a child, a family, and neighbors.

It could "hang" in an office, bringing clarity, substance, and creativity with it to prosper a business.

It could "hang" in a local church, giving inspiration to those who get to know it and encouragement to its pastor and leaders.

It could "hang" in a community center, giving light and color and bringing truth and love into a community searching for answers.

It could "hang" in an art gallery, where appreciators of art gaze on its beauty and something supernatural awakens their own creativity.

Perhaps it could be "displayed" in a state capitol building, where government officials look upon it, meet their own Creator, and are inspired to seek justice and promote truth in their work.

Or maybe it will be "seen" in a magazine, on a news rack, or online where millions gaze upon the story of its fibers and design and are spurred on to discover their own life's tapestry.

Perhaps nations will come to look at its pattern and colors and meet the One who fashioned it through the one who inspired it—*you*.

God's Crowning Achievement

Your life's tapestry is a divine creation.

You are God's masterpiece.

Are you going to let this artwork be tarnished by a world that doesn't believe? Are you going to be swayed by self-doubt that your life is not making a difference?

I persuade you to not think negatively.

Those doubts and fears are not from God. They are from an enemy who would like nothing bettcr than to undermine your success.

Kris Vallotton, Bethel Church Senior Associate Pastor, teaches, "The dogs of doom stand at the door of your destiny."

If you have a dream and something is keeping you from taking that step to achieving it, *that* is a dog of doom.

That dog has no power. He's all bark and no bite. Children of God have all power and authority to kick it out of the way. Don't listen any more. Declare you will succeed, that you cannot fail, that this is your moment to walk into your destiny, and take the step.

You Have Mighty Tools

Do you know that angels are with you, sent from God to minister to you and help you?

Do you know now that you have the mind of Christ, the ability to think supernaturally?

Do you realize the abundance you have, and that you don't need to worry about what you don't yet have?

Understand that you are dreaming with God. He had a dream when He made you, and He put it in you. He partners with you in achieving what you are called to do in this life.

Jesus tells us that the least in the kingdom is greater than John the Baptist. John the Baptist was a man who walked with God, had a supernatural birth, prophesied the coming of Christ, and was friends with and a relative of Jesus.

John the Baptist had a major role in God's plan. And you are greater. What role will you play in the unfolding of the kingdom?

You Don't Get to Keep What You Don't Give Away

Imagine you are walking down a hall of life tapestries. Amazing patterns, beautiful textures, interesting images, and striking colors greet you as you stand before each, imagining what that life must have been like and wondering how it might affect you.

Like the gifted people represented by the tapestries, God has delighted in giving you gifts, too. He has already given you many blessings. If you think back on your life, you have testimonies of what He has done for you.

There are times when He comforted, healed, and answered a prayer or when an unexpected check in the mail got you through until payday.

A "coincidence" reminded you to call a friend who needed to hear your voice at just that moment.

Or maybe He brought you someone in the form of a divine appointment, someone who helped you make a hard decision.

These stories of God's goodness belong to you.

Revelation 19:10 says, "The testimony of Jesus is the spirit of prophecy." (NKJV) That means when we tell of His goodness in our own lives, it creates an atmosphere for the same miracle to happen in the lives of those we are telling.

For example: I have had the wonderful experience of working on a ministry team at Bethel Church that prays for the sick—either over the phone or in a prayer line after Sunday services. One day I was speaking on the phone to a man from Reno, Nevada. He had back pain, and on a scale of one to ten (with ten being the worst), he told me it was at about a six.

I prayed as I normally do, seeking the Holy Spirit to come upon Him in his room and heal his back. I spoke to the muscles in his back and told them to line up and relax and be as healthy on earth as they are in heaven. (Jesus, in the prayer He taught the disciples, told us to pray, "on earth as it is in heaven." I take this literally as I pray for the sick. See Matthew 6:9-13.)

I asked the man how his back was doing. He moved around a bit and said it was down to about a five. Suddenly I saw a picture of my own experience in the

Bethel Healing Rooms when someone prayed for me, and my leg grew out to match the length of the other. This is quite a common prayer at Bethel, and I have witnessed this miracle in many places since then. But would it happen over the phone?

I told the man about this miracle that I had experienced and how it had relieved my own back pain. I asked if it would be okay if we tried it. He said it would, and I asked him if one leg was shorter than the other. "Yes," he replied. "My chiropractor has been working on that for years."

I was nervous, wondering if I should do this. A compelling urge overcame me, and I spoke to his right leg over the phone and said, "I command you to grow, now, in Jesus's name."

I waited.

There was silence on the phone.

"What's happening?" I asked.

"It's growing!" he exclaimed.

"It is?" I screamed. Even my own unbelief did not stop this miracle. We were both surprised, laughed, and joyfully thanked God.

I asked the man to get up and try to do some things that would normally make his back hurt. He walked and moved, and I could hear his emotion.

I asked him what the pain level was. "It's down to one," he gasped.

I told him to continue to walk and stretch, and as he did, the rest of his healing would come. He thanked me, and we both thanked God and hung up our phones.

I have had the privilege of praying for this miracle several more times since then. When I sense that urge from God, I know He is going to do it.

One time, a woman and her friend came forward in a prayer line. I prayed for the first woman then for her friend. It turned out the friend had a back problem. I felt the Lord say to have her friend pray for the legs.

We had the woman with back pain sit down with hips square to the back of her seat and then had her stretch out her legs as we held them. One leg was indeed almost two inches shorter than the other. I told her friend how to pray, and as she spoke the words, we all saw the leg grow out to the same length as the other. Laughter turned to tears as the two felt the love and touch of God on their lives.

Now, since I've told you these stories, I have created an atmosphere for God to do it again as the Bible verse promises. Could this happen in your life or with a friend or loved one? The answer is yes. Pray for yourself or someone else as God urges you, and see what happens.

I tell you these stories to increase your belief. I know they sound crazy to some people. A favorite poetic verse by Friedrich Nietzsche applies here: "And those who were seen dancing were thought to be insane by those who could not hear the music."[3]

I myself was suspicious when I first heard about such miracles, but my own experience increased my belief and faith; and I can't help but testify. I so want everyone to know that God is here, Jesus still heals, and Holy Spirit wants to give you a new life in the One who is your Creator. I want to proclaim from the rooftops, "It is safe to dance!"

God wants to pour out more blessing on you. He will as you take the blessings He's already given you and share them with others in whatever way you are able. That can mean helping those in need with financial gifts, it can be through healing prayer, or it can be through a kind word of encouragement to a friend.

Has God blessed you? Then bless others whom He puts in your path, and see how He gives you back even more. It's a law of the kingdom as real as the law of gravity on earth. It's here for you now.

We are His hands and feet. Will you go?

> Heal the sick, raise the dead, cleanse those who have leprosy, drive out demons. Freely you have received; freely give.
>
> Matthew 10:8 (NIV)

> Then I heard the voice of the Lord, saying, "Whom shall I send? And who will go for us?"
>
> And I said, "Here am I, send me!"
>
> Isaiah 6:8 (NIV)

How Must We Walk?

Just like our moms and dads taught us how to walk as babies, our heavenly Father has shown us how to walk His purposes out on earth. Jesus demonstrated this walk throughout His three brief years of active ministry when He healed, loved, discerned spirits, and set people free from oppression.

Using power, authority, and truth, He blasted through the negativity and unbelief of the Pharisees, and He fed the hungry with food for their stomachs and truth for their souls.

At the end of His physical life, Jesus spoke to His disciples words that still resound down through the ages to all who will believe in His name:

> Very truly I tell you, whoever believes in me will do the works I have been doing, and they will do even greater things than these, because I am going to the Father. And I will do whatever you ask in my name, so that the Father may be glorified in the Son.
>
> John 14:12-13 (NIV)

Jesus promises we will do more than Him. What did He do? He released His kingdom on earth and defeated the works of the devil. He healed all who came to Him. He did all that He saw His Father doing. He said all that He heard His Father saying.

Does that mean we, too, can do this? Yes, He said we would.

Why?

To carry on what He started and to take it to all the earth.

For how long?

Until all have heard, and He comes again.

Following are just a few ways you can begin now to equip yourself to walk in the wonderful shoes of Jesus Christ.

Wise Men Still Travel

Are you hungry to know more? Have you had a taste of new truth and life and light and love in this season, and is it compelling you to learn more? God is in your hunger. He draws us to Himself in mighty ways because He wants to satisfy our desire for more of Him. Once we have been exposed to light, the dark is no longer attractive.

My husband always reminds me that "Wise men still travel." Just as wise men followed the star on that special night of the birth of our Savior, people today are searching for Him, too.

Our hearts and spirits are crying out to know Him more.

There are so many resources for us to access. Beyond the local church, there are conferences, books, and websites that will help.

I love attending conferences. Often, Rick and I will take a vacation weekend just to go and be refreshed. We need this like we need nourishing food. These meetings offer impartation, healing, and prayer and set our feet back on the Solid Rock.

The Prophetic

Learn about prophecy. There are certain men and women called to the office of prophet, and their job is to administer that gift to the church and train others to use it. The Bible tells us that we should desire the gift of prophecy. Unlike the "office" of prophet that only certain people are called to, *prophecy* is a gift each believer has access to.

How do we use it?

It is for the building up of the church. We can ask God for words of knowledge, and He will give them to us. We can ask Him to show us how He sees a person, and He will help us to give an encouraging word and remind the person of their dreams and gifts. Prophecy is not meant to blurt out another's faults and sins. The person already knows their sins. Prophecy's job is to call out their greatness.

Do you know people who have squandered their love on the wrong people or who lust after money or fame or who dishonor their God-given gifts? Perhaps you don't really know them, but God allows you to see them by giving you a thought about them. When you declare their God-given destiny, their gifts, and tell them God's plans and dreams for them, it can be transforming.

Everyone needs encouragement. Everyone needs to be reminded of who they are. Every man, woman, and child needs to know that God has a plan and purpose for them that is good. You and I can be the harbingers of great joy for them by releasing the presence of their Creator into their day through the prophetic gift.

Sometimes people will look shocked at your words; sometimes they'll be confused. Sometimes you will see tears. Other times you may witness laughter and delight. And still other times you may have no response from them. But when you use this gift, God always shows up. Trust that, through you, God has planted something beautiful in this person.

Find Your Inmost Being

God knows you.

He knows me.

He knows our history, our future, and our coming and going.

How do we know that?

He tells us in His Word time and time again.

Here is just one place that I found it this week:

"For you created my inmost being" (Psalm 139:13).

He created our *inmost being*.

That's *who* we are. Not only did He give us our physical traits, He put His identity in us within our inmost being and personally signed it as the Creator of the universe.

Follow God's Signs

I was unpacking boxes while moving into our new rental home recently. It was just like Christmas.

Our things had been in storage since we had to move out of the home we had built and lived in for more than thirty years. Boxes had been hastily packed, and it was now more than two years since I had touched some of my favorite keepsakes.

Treasures emerged from old newspaper packing, and Rick and I gently placed them on our assortment of cherry wood shelves made by my dad, uncle, and great grandfather. Soon I came to a box of memories that included some papers from the kids' school years. I pulled out a forgotten 8 1/2 x 11 painting done by my daughter Bess when she was in eighth grade at West Grand Middle School.

In the painting I saw amazing beauty, not only in the image itself, but in the colors she used. The tree in the painting was unlike trees around where she grew up, so I wondered where she had seen this. The mountain scene also looked familiar to me, and I wondered where I had seen it.

A few days later, I knew. I looked out our living room window in Parachute, Colorado—a place I had never lived until now—and saw it. It was a beautiful mountain peak, and it looked just like the painting.

Coincidence? It was more than that. I knew God was telling me something in this. I believe He was answering the question I had posed to Him continuously in the last few months: *Why are we in Parachute, Colorado, of all places?*

His answer: *It is exactly where I want you.*

The Bible speaks of signs and wonders. They happen so often in my life today. Through art, circumstances, coincidences, Bible verses jumping out at me, and things people say to me, I have learned to recognize God's moving in my life if only to say to me, *I am with you. Keep watching. Keep praying. Things are happening now. Be ready.*

How could Bess have known or seen this coming? She couldn't have. It was God's way of using my daughter and her creativity to speak to me many years later to assure me I am where I'm supposed to be.

> Your eyes saw my unformed body
> All the days ordained for me
> Were written in your book
> Before one of them came to be.
>
> Psalm 139:16 (NIV)

I tell this story because I want to encourage you to become aware of the messages of God in your own life. Often He answers your prayers through these signs of His presence. He is your loving Father. His desire is for His children—for their protection, provision, and to help them live the life He has designed and created them for.

What a lovely and powerful God we serve!

A Blessing for You

Beloved friend, I pray you will have many of your own stories and testimonies of the goodness of God. I pray you will see and witness and feel the goodness of God in the land of the living. I bless you with powerful tools that you will use to walk in the path Jesus has commissioned you for. I bless you with a curious and hungry spirit that can't wait to learn more about your Father in heaven, who loves you with an everlasting love.

Reflect and Receive

1. Where do you hope your tapestry might hang?
2. In what ways has God blessed you? How might you, in turn, bless others through your own story?
3. How will you equip yourself today, tomorrow, and in the next year? Tell how you will proceed with these four steps:

    - Travel to where God is moving – churches, conferences, workshops.
    - Learn to encourage others through prophecy (see appendix for resources).
    - Find and share your inmost being.
    - Learn to recognize God's signs and wonders.

You Were Born to Create

> If my people, who are called by my name, will humble themselves and pray and seek my face and turn from their wicked ways, then will I hear from heaven, and I will forgive their sin and will heal their land.
>
> 2 Chronicles 7:14 (NIV)

I still can't imagine the horror it must have been for the people of 9/11 in the buildings, on the streets, and in the cities and countryside, watching the terror that seemed to never end; fearing for their lives and the lives of their loved ones; hoping for signs of life only to find death and destruction.

How do we as Christ followers respond in such disaster? Does God get the blame? How do we watch for His hand in times of crisis? How do we minister to those who are fearful and grieving?

God is still a good God, even when there is crisis, destruction, natural disaster, and war. He created a perfect world and gave it to man to govern. His will is that Earth will be like heaven—as the Lord Jesus taught us to pray. In the new covenant that Jesus came and died to birth, our understanding of God must be in the character of Jesus, who came in human form to reveal our Father in heaven. Any understanding we have of God that is not in the character of Jesus is not in line with what Jesus taught us about a God who loves, brings life, desires that no one perish, and who wants to bless.

Through one man—Adam—sin, evil, and destruction entered the whole earth. Through one man— Jesus—there is promise of redemption and reconciliation. Through the revealing of the sons of God—that's us—there is promise of the earth being healed. The creation is crying out for the children of God to know who they are.

> For the creation waits in eager expectation for the children of God to be revealed.
>
> Romans 8:19

Jesus told us that whoever we forgive, He will forgive; and whoever we condemn, He will condemn. We are partners in this governing of earth. When we rise up in intercession and stop judging and condemning and instead start forgiving and asking God to give others the favor He has bestowed on us, the healing will begin.

It's a frightening thing when the church judges a nation like Japan or a city like San Francisco with condemning remarks that "justify" God allowing disaster. Instead of condemning and judging, we need to forgive, bring mercy, and extend a hand of help and love. Do they all deserve it? No. But neither do we.

We don't know all of the answers, but we do know that God does respond to prayer, He is with us in disaster, and He is working. Again, we need to be thankful for what He is doing and has done and not focus on what He hasn't done.

On every anniversary of 9/11, I thank God that He has been revealed to our nation in mighty acts of heroism, love, mercy, protection, provision, and unity.

I thank Him for intervening in a million things we will never know about.

Finding God in the Moment

I am a hippie, just like I am a small child, an athlete, a mom, a skier, a believer, a grandma, and a woman. It is part of who I have been and a part of who I still am.

I was reminded last week of those hippie days in the 70s when I would sit and listen to beautiful music in my dorm room while watching my color light wheel making brilliant swirls on my ceiling and enjoying the musky fragrance of burning incense. Much of the music I listened to then has now become a signature for a new generation. It was and is great music.

Two of my favorite artists were Paul Simon and James Taylor. Their poetry reflected my own deep thoughts, dreams, and feelings. Their resonant voices and amazing acoustic picking encouraged my love of guitar, music, and prose. I still love their music.

So I was moved and so appreciated their presence at the tenth anniversary of the terrorist attacks at Ground Zero in New York City. As they sang, a hushed silence spoke of missed loved ones. There is something about music and poetry that creates a space for our inmost cries to be set free.

But there was something else that day that stirred me more. Prayers were restricted during the ceremony by the mayor of New York City, yet God showed Himself in astounding ways. His presence surely was at Ground Zero, in Pennsylvania, and at the Pentagon.

Did you see Him? He was there when the navy chorale sang "God Bless America" and "Amazing Grace" at the Pentagon. He was there when former president Bush honored the heroes of Flight 93 in Pennsylvania. And our Lord was standing right by President Obama when he read Psalm 46 with its comforting words for all of us:

> God is our refuge and strength, an ever-present help in trouble. Therefore we will not fear, though the earth give way and the mountains fall into the heart of the sea, though its waters roar and foam and the mountains quake with their surging. There is a river whose streams make glad the city of God, the holy place where the Most High dwells. God is within her, she

will not fall; God will help her at break of day. Nations are in uproar, kingdoms fall; he lifts his voice, the earth melts. The Lord Almighty is with us; the God of Jacob is our fortress. Come and see what the Lord has done, the desolations he has brought on the earth. He makes wars cease to the ends of the earth. He breaks the bow and shatters the spear; he burns the shields with fire. He says, 'Be still, and know that I am God; I will be exalted among the nations, I will be exalted in the earth.' The Lord Almighty is with us; the God of Jacob is our fortress.

Psalm 46 (NIV)

Belief and Unbelief

Are you, like me, sometimes an unbelieving believer?

Do you long for a time when sin does not pop its ugly head so easily in your life? When your reaction to difficulty is faith instead of fear and anger? When you expect answers to prayer and anticipate God to move in your life in miraculous ways?

I have learned a secret. It's one of those precious jewels that God hides for us, His children, to find when we search for more of Him in our lives.

It all stems down to belief.

Do we really *believe* what He says is true?

Do we really *believe* He is the healer?

Do we really *believe* He hears our prayers?

Do we really *believe* that when He died on the cross, He paid once for all of our sins for all time—past, present, and future?

Do we really *believe* that we can live in such a way to give Jesus what He paid for—all of us for all of Him—a life lived in abundance, knowing who we are in God and how much He loves us?

Do we really *believe* we can step into the promised abundant life of service that brings joy, life, and freedom to a hungry world?

If we as children of God are still struggling with sin, disease, depression, fear, anxiety, stress, unforgiveness, bitterness, and hopelessness, we have not entered the life Jesus gave everything to purchase for us.

Unbelief is the ultimate sin. Sin, no matter how big or small, is a fruit of unbelief.

We don't have to wait for heaven—we can experience the victorious, abundant life here on earth. If we want to truly believe; if we cry out like the father of the son Jesus healed, "I do believe; help me overcome my unbelief!", God will meet us and show us the way. (See Mark 9:24.)

It is in this place with God where He tells us that the work He wants us to do is to believe on the One He sent—Jesus.

> Then they asked him, "What must we do to do the works God requires?" Jesus answered, "The work of God is this: to believe in the one he has sent."
>
> John 6:28-29 (NIV)

Belief in action brings hope, healing, freedom, purpose, destiny, peace, joy, and all the wonderful fruits of the Spirit.

We are His children, adopted into His kingdom family, brothers and sisters of Christ, and heirs of all the resources of heaven. Instead of living toward heaven, we can live from heaven. Our perspective of life must be from the throne room of God.

It's a life worth jumping into—unwavering faith and total belief and acceptance in the mighty Creator of the universe, His Son, and the Holy Spirit.

> As soon as Jesus heard the word that was spoken, He said to the ruler of the synagogue, "Do not be afraid; only believe."
>
> Mark 5:36 (NIV)

> Then Jesus told him, "Because you have seen me, you have believed; blessed are those who have not seen and yet have believed."
>
> John 20:29 (NIV)

> Then Jesus said, "Did I not tell you that if you believed, you would see the glory of God?"
>
> John 11:40 (NIV)

A Blessing for You

I bless you today and for every day in the future to know who you are, whose you are, and to have an amazing sense of God's presence in your life. I bless you to discover soon that you are indeed a believing believer, finding and experiencing God in all kinds of circumstances.

Reflect and Receive

1. Think of your life today and yesterday, and project it to tomorrow. Are you aware of God's presence? Has He surprised you lately? Where is He in this moment?

2. Play some worship music today. Sing, dance, and praise Him. Listen to the words you are singing. Declare to your own spirit that you believe it all. "I am a child of God, loved and protected, provided for and blessed in so many ways." Now name some of the ways. Thankfully declare your excitement for all that God is doing in your life.

Inheritance of Inspiration

If any of you lacks wisdom, you should ask God, who gives generously to all without finding fault, and it will be given to you.

James 1:5 (NIV)

Mom thoughts: I see you, my child. You are hurting. You are wandering. You look tired. You've closed yourself up. You seem unhappy. You try to hide these things from me and put on a good, brave, front, but I know you.

When you were little, I stood on my head to make you happy (literally). When you cried, I fixed it. When you got hurt, I bandaged it. When your feelings were hurt, I read you a book, we popped some corn, and we tickled each other until it felt better. When you were sick, I made you chicken soup, bought you a magazine, and we rented a good movie.

Your heart is melded to my heart. Whether my blood runs through your veins or not, you are still my child. You always have been. God gave you to me to love and to raise, to nurture, and to teach.

So now you're all grown up. You are beautiful, handsome, physically strong, yet with gentle spirit. I am so proud of the person you have become.

But now, you have me wondering. What can I do to fix your hurt? How can I make you laugh and forget the worries of the day? I am frustrated being so far away, yet my spirit is with you. You have to feel that. Do you?

Every day my thoughts are with you and about you. I send peace and love to you through my prayers. I ask God to give you prosperity and an abundance of life's joy. I ask Him to help you know your gifts, that you might use them to joyfully and purposely fulfill your destiny.

I ask Him to protect you, to send His ministering angels to you to carry out His will in you.

I love you beyond measure. God loves you so much more. I have given you to Him, and I totally trust Him with your life.

Meanwhile, I so want you to be aware of your life. You are created for more than you now know. I pray you discover the adventure that awaits you.

If you are feeling lonely, reach out for His hand.

If you are stressed, ask Him for peace, and tell yourself to be still. You can do this. Just as Jesus commanded the raging storm and sea to calm down, and it did. You can do this with your own storms of life.

If you are angry, ask God to help you overcome and forgive.

If you are fearful, remember that Jesus taught you to not be afraid. He is with you. You can run toward crisis and trust He will help you through it.

If you are sick—mentally, emotionally, physically, or spiritually—trust that Jesus already paid a price to keep you well. He truly is the healer. Do everything you can to be healed. Seek prayer, declare His promises, and receive His healing into your body. Seek wisdom. God says when we ask for wisdom, He will freely give it. Know that God uses doctors, too. Listen to God's counsel, and be healthy and free so you can live the life He is calling you to.

If you are sad, trust that He understands. Jesus was sad, too. It is a precious human emotion. Without it, we would not know what joy means. But also understand that the kingdom, which is here on earth in your life, is made up of righteousness, peace, and joy in the Holy Spirit. Ask the Holy Spirit to come now. Feel His presence. Ask Him questions, and listen for the answers. He longs to have you enter His joy and pass it on to others. There is a joy that overcomes sadness and grief and reveals itself at surprising moments. Let go of control, and allow Him to minister to you His joy.

Precious child, your dad and I love you very much. We are so proud of you. We pray that as you have watched our lives, you have learned from us far and above what we were able to teach you verbally. We have made mistakes. Sometimes those mistakes hurt you. We are sorry and thank you for being so forgiving. We hope you have learned from the hard things we went through. We hope you have been glad in the happy things we remember as a family. Above all, know that you are our treasures, and our life's purpose is to invest in the treasure that you are. We leave you with encouragement to:

Go after your dreams.

Use your God-given gifts and talents.

Be fruitful and multiply.

Go after joy, no matter what the situation.

Live in the recognition of God's presence always.

Be generous. You don't get to keep what you don't give away.

Read your Bible and declare God's promises over you and your children daily if you can. My favorite Bible books are Psalms, John, Acts, and Ephesians. But they are all good.

Kiss and hug your kids a lot!

With love,
Mom

To all my readers, no matter what your experiences with your own parents were like, I assure you that you also have a heavenly Dad whose thoughts toward His kids are full of pride and love.

He's always in a good mood. He laughs over you, cries over you, dances over you. You are His world. You are His joy and purpose for His own being. You were created for His pleasure and friendship.

You are a spiritual creation living an earthly existence. You were in your Papa God's thoughts since before the world was made. It's only natural that you learn to depend on Him in this training ground He calls your life on earth.

He's always right there next to you. Can you sense Him?

What is Real?

I was thinking today as I was walking, that when I walk and look forward, I feel like a really skinny person. When I look at a picture of myself, I look like a chubby person. Which is real? (Very deep thoughts!)

What *is* real? From God's perspective, and looking from the spiritual realm, I am a spirit, perfectly made in God's image. That's who I am.

In the natural, physical realm, I am a human, perfectly made in God's image, and that's who I am.

So, is God chubby? Yes and no.

Is He skinny? I'd say no.

How do I know? I don't. But it was fun to think about.

The Bible says He created my inmost being. Where is my inmost being?

When I stop, and I'm still, and I focus on my body, I think I know where it is. It is somewhere behind my heart. I wonder what it is comprised of.

What did God create in there? I think it's my soul.

But what makes me, me? He put in some abilities and talents. He put in certain loves and likes. He put in certain traits like how I learn, how I think, my emotions, my sense of humor, and the way I see the world He placed me in.

What else is in there? The Bible also says He put into us a desire to find Him, a hunger to know our Creator.

> I will give them a heart to know me.
>
> Jeremiah 24:7 (NIV)

That's huge. It comes with the package when we are first formed in our mother's womb. It does not include our physical traits, although God created those, too. But this inmost being—that's the special part of us. It's where the light shines from when we first give our lives to Jesus. It's where we "rise and shine" from when we are called to bring His glory to the nations. (See Isaiah 60.) It's where He put our "salt and light." We have a flavor and a fragrance, and it comes from our inmost being. It's also the place where our praise to the Father rises from.

There is a reflection of His image in there to help us find Him. And it's the place where love is received and given and where we glow when we see it revealed in our children.

> Praise the Lord, my soul; all my inmost being, praise his holy name.
>
> Psalm 103:1-3 (NIV)

For you created my inmost being; you knit me together in my mother's womb. I praise you for I am fearfully and wonderfully made.

Psalm 139:13-14 (NIV)

The human spirit is the lamp of the Lord that sheds light on one's inmost being.

Proverbs 20:27 (NIV)

I think I'm okay with my inmost being looking chubby and my physical being looking more slender. (End of deep thinking…)

But you are not in flesh-mode, you are in spirit-mode, God's Spirit is at home in you. Anyone who does not see himself fully clothed and identified in the Spirit of Christ, cannot be himself.

Romans 8:9
(The Mirror Translation)

Swimming and Skiing Lessons

Miss Brock was relentless.

"One, two, three. Four, five, six. One, two, three. Four, five, six." I still hear her in my head forty-five years later. I hear her clapping out the rhythm as the girl's swimming class at Shorewood High School holds onto the edge of the pool, body stretched out, legs straight, toes pointed, and kicking to the "One, two, three. Four, five, six," tilting our head for a breath, then blowing bubbles in the water, legs and breathing synchronized. Woe to the person who was out of step!

The pool was cold; the swim caps and chlorine water sure to totally make our hair look a disaster for the rest of the school day. We would march through the locker room, towels around our showered body, and grab an old rag of a red or blue tank suit, freshly washed every night and used in community with a thousand other hapless girl swimmers.

I loved the class and hated the class. The only way we could get out of swimming was during "that time of the month." That's probably the only time I've ever been thankful to God for cramps and bloating.

Community showers and locker room cliques add to horrible memories forever ingrained in remote recesses of my brain.

Back to the lessons, though. In spite of my dislike for my teacher and the cold water, I did, in fact, develop a love for swimming laps—thanks to Miss Brock and my dad, who taught me a beautiful crawl in the warmer waters of Little St. Germain Lake in Eagle River, Wisconsin.

Ski lessons were my first love, though. I actually learned how to ski before I ever donned the uncomfortable laced, leather ski boots and long, straight, wooden skis with cable bindings. Channel 10 Public TV in Milwaukee offered lessons once a week in the evening.

I remember sitting in front of my heater vent at 5:00 p.m. during the cold Shorewood, Wisconsin, winter, watching an instructor teach me how to snowplow right there in my living room while chili was simmering on the stove in the kitchen.

My parents were nice. They must have seen some spark in me and knew, like I did, that I was born to ski. It would define and shape my life in many ways. In those days, I was thirteen years old and delighted when they signed me up for my first winter of Saturday lessons with the Blizzard Ski Club.

There is something good about continually learning more about what you're interested in, not only educating yourself through books and public TV, but learning from those who have gone before you, who have climbed those mountains and paid the prices through hard and good times. Those are the teachers I want for me. And that's the kind of teacher I would hope to be for others.

These are the ones who have been in the trenches. They're seasoned. They not only have knowledge from books and training, but they have wisdom that can only be born from mistakes, hardships, and sacrifice.

True Wisdom

You can tell I'm not speaking just of swimming and skiing but of life lessons. The book of Proverbs says a wise man accepts discipline (training, correction, practice) and is blessed:

> For whoever finds me (wisdom) finds life and obtains favor from the Lord.
>
> Proverbs 8:35 (NKJV)

And where do we find that wisdom?
Proverbs also says:

> When pride comes, then comes disgrace, but
> with humility comes wisdom.
>
> Proverbs 11:2 (NIV)

We receive true wisdom when we can humbly sit at the feet of one who can teach us what we don't yet know. That is when we can receive discipline and correction and thank the giver because we know it will make us wiser.

I love school. I love encyclopedias and dictionaries, and I love to sit among thousands of books in Barnes & Noble or a local library and sense the greatness in the authors. I'm in awe of knowledge. But it is only knowledge. It cannot give us wisdom.

Rick and I were talking yesterday. He had my Bible in his hand and commented on how small it was.

"It's funny," he said. "You could have the whole set of encyclopedias, and still they would not contain the wisdom that is in this one small book. It has everything we need for every situation we'll ever face."

There are many nonfiction books I read every year that teach and thrill and surprise me with their new ideas and fresh ways of thinking. These books were written by faithful authors who lived long ago and others who live now. I recognize these people as witnesses of truth and life—men and women who write from their experience, their hearts, and their own humility— knowing they gained their wisdom at the feet of others and in the pages of Proverbs, Isaiah, and the gospels.

They are quick to credit any wisdom to the revelation they receive from the Holy Spirit, Jesus, and God. They are credible witnesses of God's presence in human life and, I believe, powerfully anointed and blessed by God to deliver a message for today.

A Living Word

The Bible is forever—past, present, and future. It is a Living Word. Every time I read it, God speaks something new no matter how many times I have read that same passage. Yet, just as John the disciple said that the pages of the Bible could never contain all that Jesus did in the three years he ministered before the resurrection, so the Bible cannot contain all that God is revealing now. God will not do anything apart from His character as revealed in the Bible, but He cannot be put in a box and limited to the Bible.

How do we account for some of the ways God is revealing Himself today in gatherings around the world? There are accounts of gold dust circulating above worship teams, jewels and feathers falling from nowhere to the ground among worshipers. I have even witnessed rain falling inside a church during a holy moment of worship.

"Where is the chapter and verse for that?" you ask.

And what about those people in some of the services we see on TV—shaking, falling, and speaking in tongues? Well, there is a chapter and verse for those in Acts. That is what the 120 in the Upper Room experienced after the wind and tongues of fire interrupted their prayer service, and the Holy Spirit came on them in power.

People who saw them in the streets that morning thought they were drunk, and they couldn't understand how they were suddenly able to speak in every language of the people that had come to the city that day for the Pentecost observance.

So what about those things that can't be explained? Do we just ignore them? No. There is indeed a chapter and verse. It is Psalm 15:2: "God does what he pleases."

The early church did not have a New Testament to refer to. They did not bridle the work of God, Jesus, and the Holy Spirit. They were people just like us— astounded and amazed at their own supernatural ability to lay hands on people and see them walk, talk, see, hear, and come to life. No longer did they mourn the Jesus who died on the cross. They celebrated the Jesus who walked among them, empowered them, gave them the Holy Spirit, and taught them what God the Father looked, felt, and acted like.

These simple human beings wrote the books of the New Testament, guided by the hand of God Himself through His Spirit. The promises of the Father, the power of the eternal Creator of the universe, did not stop with the last verse of Revelation.

The Scriptures are a road map to the Father and to eternal salvation. We don't worship the roadmap; we celebrate the destination and look for it until we find it. It's the same with the Bible. God reveals Himself through it so we can find Him and celebrate Him.

What a gift!

Proverbs 25:2 says, "It is the glory of God to conceal a matter; to search out a matter is the glory of kings."

He hides nuggets of gold within His book and, like a loving parent at Easter, can't wait for us to find the wonderful treasures He has hidden for us to discover.

Why are they hidden? I like to think God, like us, loves to play, and He loves the adventure. He loves to celebrate with us when we discover one of His treasures. And there's something about seeking it out that makes us always remember it.

That's why lessons are so important no matter our age. I am so excited to be a lifelong learner. Sometimes it seems the more I learn, the more I don't know. And the more I learn, the hungrier I am for more.

There is a saying that life is not about how many breaths we take but about the moments that take our breath away.

That's how my adventure with God is. Finding those treasures are the moments that take my breath away. They're the moments when again and again I learn of the presence of a God who loves me, a Son who is my friend, and a Holy Spirit that guides me.

One, two, three. Four, five, six. Kick, kick, kick. Breathe, breathe, breathe. Reading my Bible daily is one of those disciplines that has, like swimming and skiing, resulted in a lifelong love. Every time I read my page-tattered, well-worn Bible, God's goodness is revealed, and I feel love, hope, safety, security, provision, identity, and purpose.

And I think I get a little wiser.

A Blessing for You

You have asked for wisdom. Expect to receive it abundantly. I bless you with a nature that receives truth, empowering truth, and knows what to do with it. I pray you will have divine appointments and God's hand-picked servants to surround you and train you up and pray with you as only fathers and mothers can do. God hears your cry for more of Him, and He has answered. It is time now to joyfully let down the walls and allow Him to choreograph the dance of your life with Him through hearing Him, through His words, His disciplines, His experience, and His love.

Reflect and Receive

1. Make a plan now to develop your gifts, using the wisdom from God and what He has shown you—partnering with Him in your dreams, goals, and visions.
2. Make a conscious choice now to expand your vision. What are the looming possibilities for your life? How are you changing the way you think? Who will hold you accountable?
3. Pray for understanding and ability to see the unseen world around you where angels minister on your behalf, and Jesus is always close by. Allow your spirit to be stronger than your soul (mind) as you journey.

Miracles—He is Still Creating

God did extraordinary miracles through Paul…

Acts 19:11 (NIV)

So again I ask, does God give you his Spirit and work miracles among you by the works of the law, or by your believing what you heard?

Galatians 3:5 (NIV)

Going down to a Samaritan city, Philip proclaimed the Message of the Messiah. When the people heard what he had to say and saw the miracles, the clear signs of God's action, they hung on his every word.

Acts 8:3-8 (The Message)

My book is almost finished, and I haven't even told you about many of the miracles I have witnessed.

During the past several years, Rick and I have been strongly compelled to find out if miracles truly do still happen. It's what we desired to see when we went to conferences and, finally, to school at Bethel School of Supernatural Ministry.

Although we knew there would be more we would discover, it was the report of miraculous healings that drew us. We wanted to learn how to minister healing, and we wanted to see it with our own eyes.

For years we had heard and read about testimonies in other countries. Were they real or fabricated? Could miracles really happen? God knew our desire to learn more and provided a way for us to go and experience.

What we found was amazing. Yes, we certainly saw many miracles, but that was not the main thing we left with. Though the miracles led us to a more intimate relationship with our Lord, what was most important to us was the intimacy with God we learned as a *lifestyle*.

I Am a Friend of God

Our heavenly Father truly wants to relate to us as friends and loved ones, sons, and daughters. He gently calls us to spend time with Him, just sitting with Him, quietly praying, worshiping, or even dozing. We can be in His presence. We can physically sense His Spirit. In those intimate times, He shares His purposes and ideas, transforms us into His children, and sets us on course toward total freedom in His kingdom.

Receiving His love, meditating on my identity as an adopted child, and lifting Him in worship have become part of my daily lifestyle. I walk conscious of His life in me, His power in me, and His love and compassion for me and for all those I encounter.

I pray that as I follow Him, I do what He is doing, say what He is saying, and learn to *know* God—His nature, character, personality, all of it.

What a privilege we have as Christians and how long we (and I'm speaking for myself) have neglected this great privilege. It is out of intimacy and relationship that all the miracles happen, and from that quiet and loving place that our dreams and desires, ambitions and hopes become reality in our lives.

I dream of writing books and speaking at conferences; of traveling the world and interviewing amazing people; of having wonderful relationships with my husband, children, and grandchildren; of skiing in Aspen, and owning a condo in Maui. It's okay for all of us to dream big. God, our Creator, puts those dreams in us. But they can only be reached in their fullness by knowing the Father who gives to us exceedingly abundantly more than we could ever ask or think. (See Ephesians 3:20.)

Now, about those miracles. These are just a few of what I have witnessed in the past few years.

Tijuana

We were on a weeklong mission trip with 180 students from Bethel School of Supernatural Ministry. We stayed at a retreat on the edges of the barrios of Tijuana. I had never been to a third-world country, and I have to say, I was shocked and a little frightened there as news reports warned tourists to stay away due to violence from drug cartels.

But the people were warm and accepting and eager to host us in their neighborhoods and churches. These people had nothing. They lived in lean-to shacks in ramshackle neighborhoods where roads were so unkempt that our busses would sink into deep potholes, and we'd have to get off while the drivers unstuck them.

In these neighborhoods, our groups of fifteen put on Spanish church services in small church buildings. Using interpreters, we were able to pray for many, many people during these services and on the streets of the city. Rick had a chance to work with kids, preach, and do prayer ministry. I tried my hand at prophetic art, painting pictures during worship as the Holy Spirit inspired me. I gave two of the paintings away to people in the congregation whom I felt they belonged to, and I was able to bless them with words I believe God was giving me for them. One young mother of several children tearfully accepted my painting of roses. I imagine it hanging in a special spot in a home that is sparse. I told her I felt God was showing her His love, that He saw her as a fragrant rose, and that He was bringing many blessings to her life.

God also gave me a word of prophecy for a church. This was all very new for me.

There were so many miraculous healings that happened. Following are just a few that I witnessed as I myself prayed for people.

On Revolution Street in the historic commercial and red light district, we put on a huge service of worship, complete with a band, messages of God's love, words of knowledge for healing, and invitations to receive Christ. Many gathered around the bandstand, and those of us in the crowd ministered to hundreds that night. We tangibly felt God's protection over us as we mingled on this busy street.

Back and Knee Pain Gone

One woman I prayed for with another student had been in a car accident and had much pain in her back and knee. After we prayed just a short time, she yelled out. Unsure about what happened, we prayed more then asked her to test it out. She shrieked that she was totally healed and had no pain in her back or knee.

Love Conquers Fear

A woman who had been crippled by polio was walking through the crowd in a hurry. A friend and I approached her and asked if we could pray for her. She said yes, and we prayed. Although she did not have noticeable healing, she was so mightily touched by the Holy Spirit. She bent over, weeping and hugging us. She told us her heart was healed of fear right then. She asked us to pray for her father who was ill in another part of the country. We had a powerful time of prayer. This woman taught me that the love of the Father we share in these prayers is so important—more important than the healing He brings. I always want to bring that love and compassion of Christ to every person.

Goiter Healed

Another woman in a small church my team ministered to was going through a "fire tunnel" where our team lined up in two lines and church members walked through as we touched them on their shoulders and prayed for the Holy Spirit to come and bless them. The lady passed me, and I could see she had a problem with her neck. I said a prayer for her in English as she passed by that she could not understand. But she started to shake as I said it. I found her later and asked if she needed prayer for anything. She pointed to her neck, pulling down her turtleneck shirt to reveal a massive bulge. I found a translator, and I prayed for the large goiter.

Another young man came up to pray with me, and as we both had our hands on her neck, we physically felt and visibly saw the goiter decrease in size about 50 percent. The woman was so touched and crying as we prayed for her and loved her with the compassion of Christ. Although we did not see the goiter completely disappear, God was certainly doing something. We prayed more, and I encouraged her through a translator to not give up hope and to know that sometimes healing is a process.

Love Encourages

One little girl with a severely deformed face was alone in a corner. I approached her and tried to talk with her in my broken Spanish. I said a prayer for her face, but what was remarkable about this encounter was how God just filled me with love for her and showed me how beautiful she was. I was sincerely able to tell her she was a pretty girl (una chica linda) and mean it. She did not get healed that day.

Stomach Pain Gone

I prayed for three women in one service who had stomach pain due to different ailments, and all felt the touch of the Holy Spirit. All three said their pain was gone and they felt like they were healed. One woman felt heat go through her body. I told her that was the Holy Spirit and that He was healing her. She was so moved.

Neck Receives Healing

Another woman with neck pain was totally pain free after I prayed for her. She had responded to a word of knowledge I gave at the end of the church service.

Word of Knowledge Blesses

We had been learning more about words of knowledge and were encouraged to be aware of them on our trip. On Revolution Street, I prayed and asked God to highlight someone He would like me to bless and to give me his or her name. The names Carla or Carlotta floated through my mind. I approached a group of young ladies and realized the one I thought God wanted me to talk to did not speak English, but her friend did. I asked her friend if this woman's name began with a C and what her name was. She said Claudia. Wow! That was close, and God did that!

I told Claudia that I felt like God wanted her to know she brings Him so much joy and that He loves her so much. Then I had the opportunity to talk with the whole group and found out they loved Jesus. I blessed them all and went on my way.

Freedom from Wheelchairs

We also saw people in wheelchairs get up and walk freely, rejoicing.

There were so many wonderful testimonies of salvation, healing, and people touched by God's love during our Tijuana trip.

Prophetic Art Cards Bring Hope

While on a ministry team at an Orlando Healing Conference with Randy Clark, Bill Johnson, and Dr. Mark Chironna, I was able to minister some inner healing through prophetic art. Before I left for the trip, I drew some illustrations with colored pencil on small, blank, business cards. Then I prayed that God would show me who was supposed to get these drawings and what I should say to the people.

One particular man was highlighted to me. God had even given me his name, a very unusual name, as a thought after my prayer. When I saw his nametag, I knew it was him. I walked up to him and gave him my drawing. I told him that God was thinking of him and that I had gotten a word of knowledge about neck pain and wondered if he could use some prayer. He said his neck did indeed hurt, due to a car accident. After we prayed, I found out his wife had died in that accident and also that he was about to start a new business.

I was able to pray for healing for his broken heart, favor for his new business, and just minister the compassion of Christ to him. The man tearfully thanked me and told me how touched he was that God would single him out like that.

You know what I felt after that? So blessed. God indeed gives to us in greater measure as we give to others.

Facebook

Recently I had a Facebook message from a young woman I met at that same conference. I had given her one of my drawings, too, and spoke what God had told me to say to her. In the FB note, she desperately asked for prayer for family problems. I was so delighted to pray for her again and remind her of God's promises.

Pastor On-Call Team

I was worried when I was first accepted on the Pastor On-Call team at Bethel. I loved praying for healing for people and interceding before God with them. I had loads of experience praying and loved what the Pastor

On-Call team did for people who called in from around the world. I did not take my placement on the team lightly and perhaps took myself too seriously when I told Leslie Taylor, the director, "I've never seen a miracle when I prayed for someone. You may not want me on the team."

She brushed off my comment and said I would do fine. She had mighty faith for what God could do in me. As weeks passed, she continued to teach, guide, and listen in on my calls, encouraging and commending me.

I learned through the Bethel culture and training that God *always* answers our prayers. When we pray, he is *always* doing something. Even if we don't see a result right away, we trust He is working and can confidently assure the people who we are praying for that God is blessing them.

The most important thing we minister to people, however, is not healing, but the love of God. Everyone I pray for is loved and feels loved. It's evident through their joy, tears, and brokenness before God. It's a beautiful thing to witness and participate in, whether on the phone or in person. We can lay hands on people in the natural *and* in the spiritual. God doesn't mind if we are not right there with them in person.

Restored to Life

One day while working my Pastor On-Call shift, I had a call from a pastor in Oregon. His eastern Indian accent was punctuated with concern as he told me of a friend in India who lay in a hospital, dying. "They will be taking him off the ventilator today," he said. The patient was a young Christian man with a wife and children.

Talking on the phone between California and Oregon, the two of us began praying for this man in India. I prayed and spoke life into this man. I commanded his body and soul to live and not die. I dispatched angels to the room to minister healing. I declared his body to be whole and perfect and healthy on earth as it is in heaven. I spoke hope into the people in the room with him and asked Holy Spirit to touch them all in Jesus's name. Then the Oregon pastor prayed. Soon we were taking turns, praying like Elijah prayed when He pleaded with God to end the drought, and he kept praying until he saw a fist-sized cloud in the distance. That was his answer. The rain was coming. (See 1 Kings 18:44.) The Oregon pastor and I began to declare that this man would live. It seemed as though our prayers were coming from somewhere else other than our own lips. They rose from our spirits in decrees of increasing power.

After about twenty minutes, we were done, and before we said good-bye, I asked the pastor to keep us posted.

The next day, I received a text message from Leslie Taylor asking me to come by the POC office. Instantly, I feared it was about that call and our prayer for the man in India. Had he died? Had I done something wrong? Oh, I wish I could have handed the phone to someone else. I thought, *Someone else who always has a miracle going on.*

I entered her office, anxious and on the verge of tears.

"I had a phone call from the man in Oregon you prayed with yesterday," Leslie began.

I buckled and gasped.

"What's wrong?" she asked, wondering why I was acting like that.

"What did he say?" I choked out.

"He heard from the wife of the man you prayed for. They took him off life support, and he gradually started to get better. Today he is much better, and the doctors are surprised and say he is going to be okay. He is to be released in a day or two!"

I screamed and cried and jumped and praised God at that moment. "Yes!"

The Bethel Church Healing Rooms

People come from all over the world to the healing rooms at Bethel Church, which are open every Saturday morning. There is a waiting room called the Encounter Room, where people await their turn to go into the healing room where they will have a small team of people pray for them.

I was assigned to record testimonies in the Encounter Room one day as part of the Healing Room's Testimony Team.

The Encounter Room is so fun. Literally hundreds of people are in there. There is a worship band that is a wonderful blend of acoustic guitar, keyboard, drums, violin, cello, and vocals. Their songs are spontaneous much of the time, punctuated by lyrics of healing and declarations of freedom. Healing room servants mill about, placing their hands on the shoulders of those waiting. Some servants will call out words of knowledge about ailments and conditions God is showing them He wants to heal at that moment. Those with the conditions that are called out come to the front and get prayed for, and many get healed in the Encounter Room before ever entering the Healing Room.

An Atmosphere of Divine Healing

Here is an observation I wrote while sitting in my corner of the Encounter Room one day:

Off in one corner, lovely young women and small girls are gracefully dancing to the music in flowing, princess-like dresses. In another part of the room, artists are painting images of healing given to them through prayer. Along the side of one of the walls, children are playing and coloring. At long tables sit healing-room servants who are doing prophetic drawings for anyone that wants one. The drawings are meant to encourage, strengthen, and show how God sees the person the drawing is for. There are words of hope, promise, and destiny spoken.

This is a noisy place. Many of those who have come for prayer are worshipping and dancing with the band. Others sit and read their Bibles. There are those in wheelchairs. Some of the gravely ill are lying down across chairs. Others hold babies they have brought in for healing.

Suddenly, a woman screams out in front of the band. She is now able to move her arm in a way she could not before. Another woman, a worship leader from another church, sings into the microphone, able to raise her voice in worship again—her damaged vocal chords have just been healed. From the healing room next door, there are testimonies coming continuously of multiple sclerosis healed, back pain healed, eyesight restored, and deaf ears opened.

Healing Joy

On another day in the Encounter Room, I was setting up my computer and readying myself for the day's interviews when a woman came up to me. Her husband was seated in a wheelchair in front of my table, and he was facing away from me toward the band.

She told me he was in a lot of pain, and she didn't think they could wait to be called to the healing rooms. She asked if I could pray for him. I went to him and knelt down, asking him what was wrong. He was a missionary and had returned from the mission field very sick. His heart was diseased, and he had recently had a heart attack. His body was in tremendous pain, and he was extraordinarily weak. His face was ashen, and he was bent forward at the shoulders, looking as if he was about to die. I began to pray as I had been taught. Taking authority over death and anything the enemy was doing to him, I began to speak life into his body. Something told me to pray for joy, too, so I did. Immediately, two women from the healing room's team came up to him and began to laugh. The room was quite noisy, so I know they did not hear me pray for joy over him. They laughed and laughed over him. Then they told him to start to laugh, even if he didn't want to. It became very contagious, and he started to laugh and laugh and laugh with them. I laughed, too. Soon the two lifted him from his wheelchair, and slowly, with their arms supporting him, he began to walk. They walked around and around the Encounter Room. I watched as the color returned to his face, the light shone from his eyes, his face became merry, his posture straightened, and his strength began to return.

I literally saw a man go from near death to life. It wasn't long before he was sitting at my table and giving me his testimony. He had felt joy return and something dark leave him. He knew God had touched him, and he knew his healing was complete.

The Power of the Testimony

A powerful way we helped people receive their healing during our Pastor On-Call phone calls was to ask them to remember ways God had blessed them in the past.

I remember one particular caller who was in tears. She was on her way to the vet with her aged and very sick cat. She needed prayer for her cat and for herself.

First, I asked her if God had ever answered prayer for her in the past, and, if so, to tell me about it.

It's important to tell you here that on this morning I had put together a list, as I usually did before my POC shift, which had on it several words that God had given me while I got ready at my apartment to go to the POC office. These were words of knowledge. If I had an ache in my knee, I wrote that down. If I saw in my mind's eye the color yellow, I wrote that down. If I thought of a random Bible verse, I wrote that down. It could be anything. Normally I would arrive at the office armed with about ten words of knowledge.

On this particular day, I had grapefruit on my list, which I thought was rather strange.

Now, back to my story.

In response to my question to the woman about how God had blessed her in the past, the tearful woman began to tell me how she had previously had a grapefruit-sized tumor in her uterus, and God had completely healed her through prayer.

That was all I needed. I was so encouraged, knowing that God knew this woman would call, and I would be the one to answer and pray for her. I told her about the word of knowledge and assured her God was in her situation and with her in every step she would take that day. I did pray for her cat to be healed but mostly prayed for her to have wisdom and peace.

I don't know what happened to her precious friend that day, but I do know the One who loves her most was with her and comforting her.

Warrior Angel

"Pastor On-Call, how can I pray for you?" I asked. The voice on the other end of the phone sounded fearful and alarmed, yet relieved that I had answered the call. There is something people believe about reaching a human being at Bethel Church that automatically raises their faith that God is going to do something.

The young woman, Susan (not her real name), was asking for prayer for her sister, Amy, (not her real name), who was in a Florida hospital after giving birth.

The baby was fine, but the mother was near death and in great pain, her inner organs damaged and infected after a C-section delivery.

It had been several days since the birth, and now this woman was hooked up to an array of equipment that was helping to keep her alive.

The POC team receives many calls like this for loved ones facing surgery, life-threatening disease, or death.

I shot up a prayer to my wonderful Father God, asking for wisdom on how to pray. I told this young sister on the other end of the line that the Holy Spirit was on this call with us and asked her to tell me some testimonies of how God had blessed her in the past.

Helping people remember and testify of God's goodness in their lives creates an atmosphere of faith and hope that isn't always there when we first answer the phone. Many people who call are at a point of last-ditch desperation and have all but given up hope.

The young woman proceeded to tell me of God's goodness then, surprisingly, said she felt He led her to call our office that morning through a set of strange circumstances, including seeing the word *Bethel* on a license plate.

We started to pray together. I had her begin, and then I finished. We spoke life into Amy's room and body, prayed for wisdom for the family and doctors, and commanded any evil thing in there to leave by the power of Jesus's name. I prayed that God would send His angels to surround the sickbed and minister healing to this young mother. We declared she would be healthy and able to care for her baby. Then I prayed for the loving sister, Susan, who had called. I prayed for her hands to release healing when they touched her sister, and I asked God to bless them both.

I never heard another thing about that call until about three weeks later when a friend from POC called me and relayed an amazing message.

Later, Susan called me and told me the whole story. I am still in awe of God's power and love. Following is an abbreviated version of Susan's testimony:

Doctors performed some tests on Amy, discovering her internal organs were destroyed by the infection. They surgically placed a kind of tube in the abdomen to drain fluid then closed her up. Family members surrounded the young woman and helped with twenty-four-hour care.

Susan continued to pray as we had prayed on the phone. After about two weeks, Susan was sitting in the corner of the hospital room, watching her sister sleep, when she had a powerful vision.

A huge angel stood toward the foot of Amy's bed, towering over her. He was white and gold. His teeth shone, and on the whites of his eyes she could read the verses, "I am the Alpha and Omega; it is finished," and more.

Suddenly, he drew his mighty sword and lightning and thunder exploded like a sonic boom. On the sword, the same verses were written.

Then he spread his wings and folded them over Amy. This went on for a few moments until the angel unfolded his wings and disappeared.

During this time, Amy woke from a coma-like sleep and saw her sister dazed in the corner of the room. Soon, nurses came in and saw that the young woman had awakened, and they summoned the doctors.

The following morning, a CT scan revealed the organs were completely healed and the tube that had been placed in to drain fluid had disappeared. The medical staff called it a miracle.

The young woman was soon released, and a baby and family still have their mommy.

> Are not all angels ministering spirits sent to serve those who will inherit salvation?
>
> Hebrews 1:14 (NIV)

God's Wall of Fame

After these things I looked, and behold, a door *standing* open in heaven. And the first voice which I heard *was* like a trumpet speaking with me, saying, "Come up here, and I will show you things which must take place after this."

Revelation 4:1 (NKJV)

Imagine your tapestry, hung on God's Wall of Fame. He is so proud of it. He treasures it. It waits now for you to move into your own heavenly home. Then, He will mount it on your living room wall as a reminder of your earthly journey. You will look at it and marvel, wondering how something so beautiful emerged from what you remember as a confusing time.

But then you will know what it was all about. You will begin your heavenly task. You will discover all that you were equipped with on earth as God prepared you for your eternal job.

You will finally understand as you look at the brilliant colors, the rich fibers, the textures, the dark areas, the light areas, the valleys, and mountains.

You stand back in awe as you finally get it. You remember a verse that someone always said to you when things got tough. You now know for certain the verse was always true for you.

You celebrate the fact that you never gave up hope, never turned away from the throne you knew was ahead. Look! Listen! The verse resounds in the chorus of singing angels that descends from the throne. "What the devil meant for harm, God used for good" (See Genesis 50:20).

You see in your tapestry that your heavenly Papa was always beside you. He still is. He points to a place on the tapestry where you recognize a time in your life when He seemed so far away. You see yourself. Your back is turned toward Him. You are hunched over and crying. And there He is, kneeling beside you, waiting for you to turn to Him. He is gently loving you and delivering comfort and peace.

You remember how fear had gripped your life during that dark season. But now you know it had no power over eternity. God was there. He was there. He took your hand in His and gently led you to higher ground.

He placed you in a cleft in a rock and sheltered you with His wing. He restored your strength and spoke to your heart, and in that moment, you recognized your true self in His nature. In that moment, you entered your victory, and in defeating the enemy, realized you had gained a strength, a wisdom, and an understanding you didn't have before your trouble started.

That's how He does it. That's how God turns the bad to good and the bitter to sweet.

Taste and see. He is so good!

A Blessing for You

I bless you with a letter I wrote as an assignment for ministry school. We were told to exhort and encourage a nation in a similar way that Paul the apostle wrote to the churches He founded. This was written to the people and orphaned children we ministered to in Tecate, Mexico. When I reread it recently, I discovered that this was my heart for my readers, too.

Dear Church at Tecate, Mexico,

Greetings.

You warmed my heart on our recent trip. Your special extended family welcomed us with your love, and we thank you.

I want to encourage you today that all hope is in God. All hope was released for you at the cross. God is a good God. He loves you. You who believe sit even now with Him in heaven. You are adopted into His family, brothers and sisters of Christ, and heirs to the kingdom of God. He calls you friend.

If He is for you, who can be against you? As you declare the promises of God over your town, your church, and your country, watch and see what God will do as you partner with Him in faith.

When dark days come, walk in love. Be the light on the hill that shines. When things seem hard, remember Jesus's yoke is easy. His path is hope and love and life and truth.

Are you sad? Encourage someone else, and you will feel God's pleasure.

Are you scared? Remember what Christ did for you at the cross. Step forward boldly and love someone intentionally and feel God's peace.

Is death at your doorstep? Pray a prayer of faith from your identity in Him, and watch life overcome death and light overcome darkness.

Are you imprisoned in your lifestyle? Pray to God, and He will break your chains and release you into abundant freedom.

Breathe deep.

Breathe Him.

Love, Chris

P.S. – Thank you for reading my book!

Reflect and Receive

1. What are you taking away as you finish this book?
2. How has God spoken to you?
3. Who do you know who might be helped by what you have learned?

Appendix 1

Declare the Promises of God

Author's Note: I have witnessed the power of these declarations firsthand in my own life, as well as in the lives of others I have given them to. They are anointed to transform lives, to heal, and to bring hope into every situation.

Declarations #1, (Romans 4:17; Romans 10:9-10)

These ten basic declarations are foundational to the building of your faith. They will increase expectancy of God's goodness and, thus, will increase the manifestation of that goodness in your life. Jesus said, "According to your faith, so be it" (Matthew 8:13). Say these every day for a month and see what happens to your life.

> My prayers are powerful and effective (2 Cor. 5:21; James 5:16b).

God richly supplies all my financial needs (Phil 4:19).

I am dead to sin and alive to obeying God (Romans 6:11).

I walk in ever-increasing health (Isaiah 53:3-5; Psalms 103:1-3).

I live under a supernatural protection (Ps. 91).

I prosper in all my relationships (Luke 2:52).

I consistently bring God encounters to other people (Mark 16:17,18).

Through Jesus I am 100 percent loved and worthy to receive all of God's blessings (Gal 3:1-5).

Each of my family members is wonderfully blessed and radically loves Jesus (Acts 16:30.31).

I uproariously laugh when I hear a lie from the devil (Ps. 2:2-4).

Declarations #2

Remember this: Faith is the evidence of things not seen (Heb. 11:1). Our evidence for things being true is not our circumstances but God's promises. We don't deny negative *facts* in our lives, but we choose to focus on a higher reality: God's *truth*. Faith indeed comes by hearing (Romans 10:17); therefore, we choose to speak these powerful truths to build our own faith.

I set the course of my life with my declarations (James 3:2-5).

God is on my side; therefore I declare that I cannot be defeated, discouraged, depressed or disappointed (Rom 8:37; Psalms 91; Phil 4:13).

I am the head, not the tail. I have insight. I have wisdom. I have ideas and divine strategies. I have authority (Deut. 28:13; Deut. 8:18; James 1:5-8; Luke 10:19).

As I speak God's promises, they come to pass. They stop all attacks, assaults, oppression, and fear from my life (2 Peter 1:2-4; Mark 11:23-24).

I have the wisdom of God today. I will think the right thoughts, say the right words, and make the right decisions in every situation I face (James 1:5; 1 Corinthians 2:16).

I expect to have powerful divine appointments today to heal the sick, to raise the dead, to prophesy life, to lead people to Christ, to bring deliverance, to release signs and wonders, and to bless every place I go (the book of Acts).

I expect the best day of my life spiritually, emotionally, relationally, and financially in Jesus's name (Romans 15:13).

Declarations #3

One of the main methods Jesus and the apostles used (in the gospels and Acts) was to *speak to* things. You will notice that they did not ask God to heal people, to cast out demons, or to raise the dead, but they spoke to bodies, to demons, to the wind, etc. Jesus encouraged us to speak to mountains in Mark 11:23. This set of declarations focuses much on our speaking to the various aspects in our lives.

> I have a covenant with God, and by the blood of Jesus I release my divine protection and divine provision (Hebrews 8:6).

> My angels are carrying out the Word of God on my behalf (Psalm 103:20).

> Any adversity, attack, accidents, and tragedies that were headed my way are diverted right now in Jesus's name (Psalm 91).

> I speak to the raging waters in my life, "Peace, be still." I say to my mind, "Peace, be still." I say to my emotions, "Peace, be still." I say to my body, "Peace, be still." I say to my home "Peace, be still." I say to my family, "Peace, be still" (Mark 4:39).

> Now I speak to every mountain of fear, every mountain of discouragement, every mountain of stress, every mountain of depression, every mountain of lack and insufficiency, and I say, "Be removed and cast into the sea in Jesus's name" (Mar 11:22-24).

> And I speak to this day, and I call you blessed. And I declare that I serve a mighty God who today will do exceedingly and abundantly beyond all that I can ask or think (Eph. 3:20). I say you are a good God, and I eagerly anticipate your goodness today.[4]

Appendix 2: Books and Resources

Dreaming with God by Bill Johnson
Born to Create by Theresa Dedmon
When Heaven Invades Earth by Bill Johnson
Money and the Prosperous Soul by Stephen DeSilva
The Happy Intercessor by Beni Johnson
The Supernatural Ways of Royalty by Kris Vallotton
Basic Training for the Prophetic Ministry by Kris Vallotton
Cracks in the Foundation by Steve Backlund
Dream Culture by Andy and Janine Mason
Living From the Unseen by Wendy Backlund
www.ibethel.org–Bethel Church website

www.ibethel.tv–Bethel Church online sermons and conferences

www.bssmadventures.blogspot.com – Christine Tracy's blog

www.christinetracy.com

Appendix 3

Simple Prayer of Salvation:

Lord Jesus,

Take my sin, take my life, take my past and my future; I give them freely to you. I want to change. I want the abundant life You promise. I am sorry for not living a life that honors you. Thank you for dying on a cross to pay the price for my sin so I may live with You in eternity. I believe. And I receive all that you have for me now. Amen.

The Lord's Prayer

In this manner, therefore, pray:
Our Father in heaven,
Hallowed be Your name.
Your kingdom come.

Your will be done
On earth as it is in heaven.
Give us this day our daily bread.
And forgive us our debts,
As we forgive our debtors.
And do not lead us into temptation,
But deliver us from the evil one.
For Yours is the kingdom and the power and
the glory forever. Amen.

Matthew 6:9-13 (NKJV)

The Apostles' Creed:

The basic creed of Reformed churches, as most familiarly known, is called the Apostles' Creed. It has received this title because of its great antiquity; it dates from very early times in the church, a half-century or so from the last writings of the New Testament.

I believe in God, the Father Almighty, the Maker of heaven and earth, and in Jesus Christ, His only Son, our Lord:

Who was conceived by the Holy Ghost, born of the virgin Mary, suffered under Pontius Pilate, was crucified, dead, and buried;

He descended into hell.

The third day He arose again from the dead;

He ascended into heaven, and sitteth on the right hand of God the Father Almighty; from thence he shall come to judge the quick and the dead.

I believe in the Holy Ghost; the holy catholic church; the communion of saints; the forgiveness of sins; the resurrection of the body; and the life everlasting. Amen.

Endnotes

1   Beni Johnson, *The Happy Intercessor*, (Shippensburg: Destiny Image, 2009), 30-31.

2   Daniel Vogler, *Revival Lifestyle*, "http://www.revivallifestyle.com/macbook-testimony/." Accessed November 4, 2012.

3   Friedrich Nietzsche, http://www.goodreads.com/author/quotes/1938. Friedrisch_Nietzsche (accessed November 5, 2012).

4   Backlund, Steve. *Steve's Life-Launching Declarations List*. http://ignitinghope.com/declarations/ (accessed November 5, 2012).